To Luciano
With the hope ...

Christmas 2005

Mud, Straw
and Insults

Mud, Straw and Insults

CONFESSIONS OF AN HONEST ESTATE AGENT

ROY BROOKS

JOHN MURRAY
in association with

Roy Brooks

Text © Roy Brooks Ltd 1985
This selection 2001

First published in Great Britain in 2001 as *Brothel in Pimlico*

This edition published in 2004 by John Murray (Publishers)

Illustrations pages 1–63 and 74 © David Eccles
Pages 64–112 © Diana Durrant

Edited, designed and formatted on computer by John R Murray

The right of Roy Brooks to be identified as the Author of the Work
has been asserted by him in accordance with the Copyright,
Designs and Patents Act 1988.

1 3 5 7 9 10 8 6 4 2

A CIP catalogue record for this title is available from
the British Library

ISBN 0 7195 6779 3

Printed and bound by
Creative Print and Design (Wales), Ebbw Vale Gwent

Hodder Headline policy is to use papers that are natural,
renewable and recyclable products and made from wood grown in
sustainable forests. The logging and manufacturing processes are
expected to conform to the environmental regulations of the
country of origin.

John Murray (Publishers)
338 Euston Road
London NW1 3BH

Mud, Straw and Insults

Roy Brooks was an eminent estate agent who became a national figure, mostly for one enduring reason: because of the puckish delight he took in telling the truth, the whole truth – and even the unwholesome truth. In a trade well known for its euphemisms, optimistic clichés and skilful literary camouflage, he won the delighted applause of the property-buying and advertisement-reading public.

He died in 1971 leaving behind him an extraordinary collection of advertisements. His honesty and impudent originality were, surprisingly perhaps, rarely offensive. He walked his editorial tightrope with a natural flare and disarming humour. He espoused causes, advocated charities and benefited both. He brought a nationwide following to the *Sunday Times* and the *Observer* and readers who seemed no less attracted to his political and social homilies than to his scathing and acid descriptions of property.

[The above is taken from the introduction by David Wilcox to the original edition.]

Roy Brooks' advertisements were originally presented in two slim volumes – *Brothel in Pimlico* and *Mud, Straw and Insults* – both of which are long out of print. This present volume contains the best of both.

*

The Roy Brooks agency still operates from prominent offices in South London (contact 020 8299 3021). The present owners treasure Roy Brooks' legacy, and have evolved his plain-speaking, down-to-earth honesty into a contemporary approach that remains distinctly personal.

Illustrations by
David Eccles
[pages 1–63 & 74]
and
Diana Durrant
[pages 64–112]

CURZON PLACE, quiet cul de sac off PARK LANE. Facing Sth., luxurious bachelor apartment of bearer of a famous name (which may not be disclosed) who, having tried his hand as film extra, stockbroker, school master & tutor to a Maharajah is getting married & must sacrifice albeit at far, far below the £2,000 he has, this year, lavished on this noble Georgian Mansion's 1st flr. flat with 32ft. drawing room opening onto balcony, a charming bow window, 2 good bedrms., rich red carpeting to lux. bathrm. & lav., super-fit. kit. Lift. Pres. lse. to Sep. 1966 ONLY £850 p.a. inc. rates.

FASHIONABLE CHELSEA, Lamont Rd. Do not be misled by the trim exterior of this modest Period Res. with its dirty broken windows; all is not well with the inside. The decor of the 9 rooms, some of which hangs inelegantly from the walls, is revolting. Not entirely devoid of plumbing, there is a pathetic kitchen & 1 cold tap. No bathrm., of course, but Chelsea has excellent public baths. Rain sadly drips through the ceiling on to the oilcloth. The pock-marked basement flr. indicates a thriving community of woodworm; otherwise there is not much wrong with the property. In the tiny back garden an Anderson shelter squats waiting.... Lse. 40 yrs? G.R. £50. SACRIFICE £6,750.

CHESTER SQ. BELGRAVIA. Under its mantle of dust & dirt this is a very fine house; there is even an air of aristocratic decay about the broken passenger lift. *"I'm afraid the lift is out of order we'll have to walk up ..."* cannot fail to impress your guests. 5 principal bedrms., 2 staff rms., plus 3 attic rms., magnificent, vast "L" shaped 1st flr. drawing rm., about 35 ft., fine large dining rm., solid mahogany doors, study, a frightful old kit., 3 old fashioned bathrms. I suspect that under the grime, this eminent Banker's house is pretty sound; but better get a good surveyor. LONG 41 yr. lse. G.R. ONLY £100 p.a. Say, £19,995 but try any offer; owner might take a low price from deserving, but impecunious, young couple. Viewing Sunday 3–5. Knock 4 times.

DARKEST PIMLICO. Seedy FAMILY
HOUSE two rooms in basement, ground, 1st
& 2nd floors and attic rm. on 3rd. Decor!
peeling, faded and fly blown. Garden – good
for Westminster – all of 20ft. Lease 80 yrs.
G.R. £60 p.a. £6,950. If you are too late to
secure this gem we have a spare along the
road rather more derelict. A lightly built
member of our staff negotiated the basement
stair but our Mr. Halstead went crashing
through.

OPULENT 18TH CENTURY SETTING, FASHIONABLE ISLINGTON. NEWLY BUILT SUNNY 2nd. floor LUX. FLAT looking out over the lovely ancient trees and remnants of the aboriginal inhabitants quietly fishing in the canal which peacefully meanders through tended gardens of the well-preserved well-heeled intellectuals' neighbouring properties. BALCONY. 25ft. drawing rm, 2 bedrms., 2 mod. bathrms. Well fit. kit. Lse. 90 yrs. G.R. £45. £8,500 even try offer.

FASHIONABLE CHELSEA. Immaculate (protected) period res. of Colonel – late Heavy Foot & winner of Beau Brummel award (now framed in the downstairs lav.) shifting his moorings to be nearer his yacht. A superb 26ft L-drawing rm., sun pours in: windows both ends. Richly comfortable dining rm.; the elegant decor setting off paintings & scale model of his Folkboat which is owned with all the panache of a 12 metre. An air of exquisite refinement broods over the splendid master bedrooms., 2 other good bedrms., mod. bathrm. shower. One of the best kitchens I've seen. Maritime decor, of course. Gleaming parquet. Delightful little garden. Good parking in this little cul-de-sac. Good lse. G.R. ONLY £23.15 p.a. SACRIFICE £9,850. Even try ANY offer.

SCOTT OF THE GUARDIAN asks us to sell his elegant & historic George II, circa 1759. residence in CHEYNE WALK, CHELSEA: an address that immediately stamps you as a person of wealth & even – by sympathetic magic – of culture. A few doors from TURNER'S house, that fellow who always got home after a night on the loose, by sticking a fiver in the heel of his sock, to paint those magnificent sunsets. You've the same superb river view. Suitably magnificent 30 ft. dble. drawing rm., dining rm., study or 6th bedrm., 5 dble. bedrms., mod bathrm., well fit kit. Decor in impeccable taste. BARGAIN £27,750 FREEHOLD.

9

IT WAS NICE OF THE FOR-
TUNATELY INDESTRUCTIBLE MR.
STIRLING MOSS to make a generous
reference to us apropos his Nassau house
in last week's SUNDAY TIMES: but
I do hope this will not bring a spate of
outlandish properties like the disused light-
house off the Irish coast etc. etc. ALAS it is
ONLY IN THE LONDON AREA that we
can, & will, sell or let anything. ROY
BROOKS.

TELY STAR T*RR*NC* M*RG*N, whose
Francis Drake is now a hit on American
Tely, illustrating, no doubt, that we were
able to lick Spain without spontaneous
combustion – or Mr. Randolph Hearst.
SACRIFICES his cosy HUGH ST. WEST-
MINSTER modernized period res. suitable
for smallish couple (the rooms are not
large) who, as he says: *"can shop cheaply
in Vauxhall Bridge Road & flit at night in
evening dress into Belgravia."* 3 dble. bedrms.,
drawing rm., dining rm., new 1st. flr. kit.,
mod. bathrm. – both need a lick of paint.
PLUS s/c BASE FLAT let furnished 7 gns.
p.w. Lse. 86 yrs. at £80 p.a. £9,250.

MUSCLE MAN, weight-lifting champion
& photographer of pin-ups offers his elegant
little top flr. (7th) FLAT. FASHIONABLE
ST. JOHN'S WOOD. Drawing rm., balcony,
dble. bedrm. tiled bathrm., mod. kit. LIFT.
Perfect: quiet & sunny. Baby forces move.
Lse. 5 yrs. ONLY £420 p.a. low offer f. & f.

FASHIONABLE FULHAM *"You think
this house is beautiful – wait until you see the
photographs,"* they said and, smiling from
the pages of a Glossy is the Colonel (The
expelled British Military Attache in Algeria)
and graduate of the Rank Charm School, the
progenetrix of his 3 children, posed on the
stairs of their Edwardian Res., reconstructed
to the highest Belgravia standards. NEW
OIL CENTRAL HEATING. Elegant drawing rm. opening thro' arch to dining rm.,
study or playroom for soirees. 3 dble. bedrms., mod. bathrm., well fit. kit. Garden.
Decor excellent. BARGAIN: ONLY £9,995.

CHILDREN'S SURGEON, joining the Freemasons & going into the City, as a sort of medical missionary, to tend sick business men (*"Poor Dr. Faustus,"* said a wise old doctor friend of mine, and one of them; *"a millionaire at 40 – & dead at 42"*). Anyway, MUST SACRIFICE rather grand MOCK GEORGIAN det. SUTTON house. 5 bedrms., 4 big. 1 only just makes the grade as a bedrm., bathrm., principal lav. with throne in green brocade, lounge hall, drawing rm. which can be opened into dining rm. (32ft.) for entertaining, b'fast rm., lab.-sav. kit. 52 power points. BIG GARAGE. BIG GARDEN with fountain & fish pond – sadly depleted, however, by patients of nearby veterinary surgeon. Country air. 29 mins. Victoria. £8,995 FREEHOLD.

ST. PETER'S VILLAS, ST. PETER'S SQ., W.8. An address which places you among the creme de la creme. Stricken by the freeze & *"Govt's broken promise to us"* (Like many other doctors he's still running his old Mk. VI – it's the spivs & pop singers who can afford the S.3's) our client MUST SELL enchanting REGENCY HOUSE. Thousands spent, original Adam features. Super dble. drawing rm. Cosy dining rm. Study or 4th dble. bedrm. 3 other bedrms. mod. bathrm. super kit. £14,995 FREEHOLD.

SEMI-GLOSSY MAG. EDITOR, WRITER & WORLD RANGING V.I.P. JOURNALIST (He has even had an invitation to Buckingham Palace – marked " Tradesman's Entrance") offers his new ('58) house, which, with resident poodle (*" Reluctant to leave"*) much photographed for Ads. with real artificial flowers stuck in front garden. Sparkling all white decor, spacious drawing rm., abt. 24ft. Dining alcove. Well fit. kit., big larder, 3 decent bedrms., mod. tiled bathroom. GARAGE. Some of the most refined neighbours in LAMBETH, within earshot of Big Ben, walking distance of House of Commons & hard by an all night launderette. Small back gdn., lawn & cherry tree – all this for a mere £4,995, even try offer. Lse. 995 yrs. G.R. Only 8 gns.

FASHIONABLE CAMPDEN HILL. LUX. FLAT WITH LOVELY LITTLE GARDEN. Thousands spent by gentle-woman creating haven of rest after 10 yrs. cruise on husband's 80 ton luxury yacht in med. *"Seen only thro' the galley porthole ..."* Fine spacious drawing rm., dble. bedrm., new bathrom., well fit. kit. Lots of sun. Lse. 43 yrs. G.R. £70. ONLY £4,995.

N.10. CLOSE HIGHGATE WOODS. The Edwardian abode of Gentleman Lec-turer on Psychology & Lady Child Psychol-ogist. The children of this union *"Climb over the fence, gambol on the grass & pick pounds of blackberries – can't see a house: in summer you have"* she says, *"the illusion of living in the country."* Ent. Hall, comfortable drawing rm., dining rm. semi open plan to well fit kit. 4 bedrms., mod. bathrm. FREEHOLD £7,495.

£4,995 FREEHOLD. The Smooting, mod. architect blt. (circa 1954) res. of OLIVER, the Cambridge scientist son of my old friend the late TOM WINTRINGHAM, the " English Captain" who found Franco in Spain. 3 bedrms., one as study which, poised on the rim of KNAPP HILL nr. Woking, commands a rather splendid vista to the distant wooded hills. Pleasant booklined sit-ting rm., dining rm. with French window to garden, with flowers and sandpit and nice inaccessible jungly bit at end. Mod. b & k. *"Outside"* says wife, a Viking lady, *"It's very English – leaded lights. Inside"* she adds, peer-ing thro' the Venetian blinds, *"it's very Dan-ish ..."*

W1. Small modernised PERIOD RES. Dble. drawing rm., 3 decent enough bedrms., b. & k. (new 8 years ago). Small paved garden with flower bed. The outlook – the backside of Woolworths – might be considered a little fustian, but, good enough for our clients (HER grandpa & uncle are Peers: descended from DUCHESS OF DEVONSHIRE. HE, decent upper middle class, descended from 6 generations of Generals. STIRLING CASTLE was *"Home"*), it's probably good enough for you. £8,550 FREEHOLD.

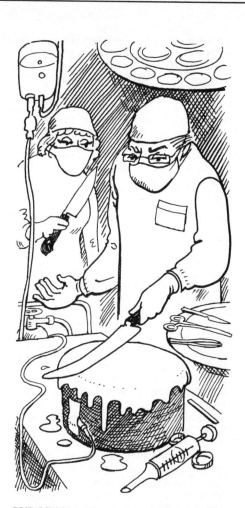

SURGEON'S FLAT in fashionable (1958) neo-Georgian block where persons of title mingle democratically with the medicos. Home of brilliant **BRUDENELL THE KNIFE** (obtainable in stainless steel, double bladed and equally adaptable for icing the cake – or biopsy). With delightful disregard for cash he's refused to patent it; in the interest of humanity. Lots of sun & near Heath. 3 DBLE. bedrms., drawing rm., mod. tiled bathrm., large kit. Lovely gardens. GARAGE. Blackheath's loss is Bradford's gain – he's going to the Paris of the north & MUST SELL. ONLY £4,950. Lse. 98 yrs. G.R. ONLY £18.

JAMES DUFUS OF DALCLAVER-HOUSE, gentleman, offers his elegant 3rd. flr. CHEYNE ROW CHELSEA FLAT, which has gone up in the world since CARLYLE, opposite, complained of his neighbours' chickens. Drawing rm. of great dignity with electric lights points for family portraits, which can be obtained in the Fulham or King's Rd. 2 bedrms. fit. wardrobe for kilts, mod. b. & k. Lse. 95 yrs. G.R. ONLY £50. £5,550 TRY OFFER. Little enough for an address that sets you apart from the common herd.

RETURNING TO CANADA. Film Director and little shepherdess from The Roman Spring of Mrs. Stone, sacrifice for immediate sale, this solid PUTNEY bourgeois family res. which they have transformed into what she describes as *"A pretentious little house."* Complete with NEW OIL CENTRAL HEATING and bathrm. in the American taste; new tub, Beardsleys on the wall, black curtains and a chandelier (also, of course, a chandelier in the w.c. – and room for 2nd bathrm.). A gorgeous BIG drawing rm., fine dining rm., 5th bedrm. or Montage rm., b'fast rm. new kit., 4 perfect bedrms. The principal bedrm. is a splendid 25ft. affair in ersatz Adam style. Interesting garden. £6,990 FREEHOLD.

IMPORTANT YOUNG GENTLEMAN (he tells me he appeared with his mum – a Mme. Vicani, on This Is Your Life) going to New York in connection with new glamour mag. for Men – PLAYBOY – and must part with 7th flr. MOD. BLOCK FLAT. Fairly spacious recep. rm., 2 bedrms., mod. tiled b. & k. CENT. HEAT. c.h.w. lift. Lse. 7 yrs. from last Sept. ONLY £325 p.a.

GURTH KING HAROLD'S KID BROTHER – heavily armoured in brass curtain rings (B.B.C. 2.) Offers his elegant, fashionable CHELSEA 1st flr. FLAT so spacious, you can isolate the guests. Delightful 23ft. drawing rm. French windows to balcony. Unusual dining rm. divided to make 4th bedrm. Mod. bath. & kit. Decor gd. Lse. 31½ yrs. G.R. ONLY £50. £9,995.

SOLICITOR, respected editor of Legal Periodical & restless girl model forced to leave their ISLAND PARADISE at THAMES DITTON & interesting neighbours "Coming back from the Swan" he says, *"Strangers in the night like the lady carrying her clothes in a bundle & muttering how it all began in the Scampi bar ...."* 60ft. RIVER FRONTAGE & o'lking Hampton Court Park. Delightful 26ft. dble. drawing rm., fine kit. dining rm., 3 dble. bedrms., lux. bathrm. Delightful garden, immaculate throughout. Lse. 95 yrs. G.R. £30 p.a. £7,995.

WESTMINSTER ABBEY CHOIR BOY AT QUEEN'S WEDDING sits at piano thinking of his next pop number. Gracious drawing rm., which might be in a rich country rectory, bucolic outlook over CLAPHAM COMMON. Exquisite dble. bedrm., a simulacrum of a medieval tent richly coloured drapes to wall & ceiling. Housekeepers bedrm., lux. coloured bathrm & kit. £28 per week income from Dr. in base. & refined bedsitters upstairs. £9,995 FREEHOLD.

FASHIONABLE DULWICH. Dr. must quickly sell new (59) SUPER-LUX. Architect blt. RES. as wife taken to Action Painting – keeps introducing new materials – earth, sand ... Elegant 30ft. drawing rm, pol. wd. flr. delightful b'fastrm./kit. 3 fine bedrms. one to balcony, lux. tiled bathrm. GARAGE. Gdn. apple & pears, roses. ONLY £6,550.

"THEY DRANK THE GAY BUBBLY IN ECCLESTON SQ." Wrote SAKI in 1912 in his novel of English upper-class collaborators prophesying German aggression. A RATHER SPLENDID PENTHOUSE in this noble garden sq. with TENNIS. Spacious drawing rm., picture window sliding back to sunbathing terrace; principal dble. bedrm., 5ft × 6ft. Pygmy bedrm.; the only snag: *"access only through our bedrm."* says top Ad. man who did those wonderful Army recruiting ads., as well as being against The Bomb, now turned Anthropologist. Lease 86 yrs. G.R. £80 p.a. Only £4,400.

£5,750 FHLD. *"I bought this house off Wandsworth Common for its quiet solidity, warmth & comfort. 15 mins. Town,"* said client from Th' North who has spent £2,000 on restoring this double fronted semi. to its Victorian prime. *"To house my Victorian treasures .... have to entertain a lot of foreigners, like to show them British way of life. I'm Chairman of the Conservative Party ..... Still play cricket ... There's a fine bust of Wellington on the landing ..."* Commodious & comfortable drawing rm., gd. dining rm., smoking rm. or 5th bedrm., 4 dble. bedrms., fit. wdrbs., 1 basin, new b. & k. Garden.

EXCITING, STIMULATING, EALING.
Former home of Royalty & Prime Minister
PERCIVAL (an old print of mine depicts him
as an ass: *"Famed for doing all the drudgery &
dirty work of the House ... very mild in his
disposition."* But this did not, of course, pre-
vent him being murdered.) Whilst this det. &
spacious FAMILY HOUSE (circa 1900) is
for a person of lower station: a solicitor,
doctor or accountant, it has all the comforts
peculiar to the middle classes. Mod. bathrm.
with shower, well fit. kit. 6 bedrms., 5 dble.
Ample drawing rm., dining rm., study. Large
garden. GARAGE. ONLY £7,550 FREE-
HOLD & try any offer as empty & anxious.

KENSINGTON CT. PLACE. W.8. Scion
of distinguished ancient Liberal family
(Uncle Bryant held Lambeth all his life) outgrown FABULOUS FLAT on which he has
lavished thousands. Mr. D. Hicks the decor-
ator has done a perfectly splendid job. Bookshelves contain real leather-bound books. A
kind of legal air hangs abt. the vast studio-
type, chandelier-lit drawing room; with gallery (for extra sleeping), Principal bedroom
just takes four-poster, and 2 attic bedrooms.
Air of rich luxury abt. bathroom with its
interesting prints. Well fitted kit. lse. $3\frac{1}{2}$ years
at only £190 p.a.

A FACE FROM THE PAST; now minus
its beard, reminds me of my distinguished
client's original letter some years ago; *"It was
pointed out to me that it would be a Good Thing
to buy and convert a big house into flats. It has
been a good thing for my Architect, Surveyor,
Builder, Accountant, Solicitor ..."* He shld.
have consulted us earlier: the poor fellow
made a modest loss. ANYWAY he's now
offered us a fine ENT. FLR. (Up steps like
1st flr.) SUNNY HAMPSTEAD FLAT, Imposing 29ft drawing rm., dining rm. or 4th
bedrm. 3 other gd. bedrms., 2 mod. bathrms.
Steeped in culture – fellow tenants inc. famous playwright, an Air Marshal, 2 leading
novelists & an OBE. The owner's wife is
herself a prize winning romantic Novelist
(*"You get high marks for chastity"*) said the
judge.) A 10 yr. lse. for ONLY £2,850 – equal
to ONLY £285 p.a.! Peppercorn rent.

DEVOUT SOCIALIST SOLICITOR & S. AFRICAN GIRL NATIONALIST sadly eschew the rich luxury of their sparkling, mod. Maida Vale PENTHOUSE STUDIO FLAT. Gorgeous Studio drawing rm. with gallery has 20ft. window! Sunbathing roof gdn. for open air lovers. 2 bedrms., lux. tiled bathrm., super fit. kit. exquisite decor. CENTRAL HEATING. C.H.W. LIFT – THE LOT. Suit film star or Solicitor who has done well in the property market. Lse. 7 yrs. ONLY £400 p.a. SACRIFICE FAR BELOW COST.

EDGE HILL, WIMBLEDON, high & not far Common, nr. FASHIONABLE R.C. Church The Lux. newly blt. (3 yrs. ago) 1st & 2nd flr. mais. of lady missionary to darkest PERU & other parts of S. America who, like me, thinks that the spread of literacy & food & – by small doses – of interdenominational simple Christian principles, is more important than even space tely. Lovely 22ft. drawing rm., 2 gd. bedrms., tiled bathrm., well fit. kit. Decor only fair. GARAGE. ONLY £4,995. Lse. 97 yrs. G.R. ONLY £20.

FASHIONABLE HAMPSTEAD, N.W.3. Sunny 1st. flr. FLAT. Airy Drawing rm. 2 DOUBLE bedrms. well fit. kit. Bathrm. where Chartered Accountant and American wife brew beer in the bath *"like her dad did in San Francisco – except he made Gin ..."* Lse. 39 yrs. G.R. ONLY £25 p.a. ONLY £5,750 & try any offer.

EMPIRE BUILDER (*"I left after my friend put Independence Badge which Tanganyikan Govt. issued on his dog's collar ..."*) GOING S. AFRICA & MUST SELL *"Mawingo"* New architect blt. '64. *"Visitors"*, he says, *"are awed by its beauty & luxury."* BEAUTIFUL BICKLEY, 12 miles TOWN. In beautiful EASY garden. *"Planted nothing that won't stand up for itself."* Gorgeous 23ft drawing rm. dining rm., study, 4 DBLE. bedrms., 2 lux. bathrms., SHOWERS. Gold fits. Super Kit. Dble. GARAGE. worth over £20,000. He'll consider any offer on £15,500 FREEHOLD as he's yearning for Sun & Freedom.

SHE WAS ONLY A TEA-TASTER'S DAUGHTER who, passing through a remount depot, became a can-can dancer and dental receptionist and, finally came to roost in this FASHIONABLE CHELSEA SQ., and whose lovely home we are privileged to offer. DIVIDED as: ent. Flr. mais. – 2 dble. bedrms., 2 rec. opening into one gorgeous 35 ft. rm. for receptions, large bathrm., kit. Fit. carpets inc. Small garden. 1st flr. as STUDIO FLAT – own b. & k.-dining rm. Upper mais. – 2 dble. bedrms. large rec. rm., mod. b. & k.-dining rm. Pres. lse. to Aug. '73. ONLY £200 p.a. BARGAIN £5,990. HUGE INCOME POTENTIAL.

MAGNIFICENT, HISTORIC 1st FLR. FLAT in: *"The prettiest house in England. What addition to happiness could you desire? A pleasant house & garden, fine air, beautiful food, a sweet tempered young lady to ..."* wrote GENERAL WOLFE of his home; since had accolade of mention in THE QUEEN. All windows command BLACKHEATH or GREENWICH PK. Gorgeous 22ft. drawing rm., circular bay, 3 dble. bedrms., lux. bathrm., lab. sav. kit. Lse. 48 yrs. G.R. ONLY £25. ONLY £5,950, try any offer as client taking Squadron to Singapore – pity we hand't one to send 20 yrs ago.

THE SPLENDID HYDE PARK SUNNY 3rd flr. flat (lift) of failed Theatrical Designer, kitchen operative & opulent collector of bois clair furniture. Impressive entrance hall, 2 LARGE reception rms., 2 dble. bedrms., 2 bathrms., 1 super new lux. shower, vanitory unit & extensive wall mirrors, American kit. super ckr. & spit. Pres. lse. to Sept 1975, abt. £550 p.a. Mod. fig. val. f & f.

19

WENDOVER COURT, FINCHLEY RD. Sunny 2nd. flr. FLAT in MOD. BLOCK, yet already eminent residents. Plaque to C. B. Fry. (This was brought to us by a highly placed Englishman who was the first to contact Maclean & Burgess in Russia – If you see a bearded hunchback in blue-tinted spectacles viewing the flat, who straightens up before entering a black limousine, she is probably from MI5.) Decent sized panelled ent. hall. CENTRAL HEATING. dble. drs. to spacious drawing rm., ideal for receptions. Dining rm., 3 bedrms., tiled bathrm., gd.-sized kit. LIFT. 7 yrs. lse. ONLY £600 p.a. SACRIFICE far below cost; v. mod. fig. to inc. f & f.

FASHIONABLE HIGHGATE. Rich Tycoon eschews family business for abstract Art & St. Ives (this one said it didn't matter which way up his pictures were hung – & why not? After all a pretty woman looks just as good upside down.) Circa '04: it's got an ugly face but lovely light big rooms inside. NON-BASE RESIDENCE. Split-level double drawing rm., abt. 30ft., study or extra bedrm., gd. dining rm., 5 gd. bedrms, fine new kit., tiled bathrm. with shower. 3ft. double STUDIO with large top light. £8950 FREEHOLD, even try offer.

OFF FASHIONABLE HOLLAND PARK AVENUE. Alleged development area. PERIOD RESIDENCE modernised 10 yrs. ago for the Ban the Bomb Cellist Joy Waller (*"bit squarer though than my musical namesake"*) Big dble. drawing rm., 3 gd. bedrms., b & k. plus *"rear"* good sized STUDIO – door to Pottery Lane. Decor not too bad as you enter: gets worse as you go up. £4,995 FREEHOLD.

REGENT'S PARK ROAD. Old Etonian's scruffy Period res. overlooking **PRIMROSE HILL & ST. PAUL'S.** Self-styled *"Rejected Poet & Painter."* (It's always possible to tell an English gentleman from the lesser breeds. The latter boast of their successes, the former speak only of their failures. Our distinguished client has attempted, unsuccessfully, to paint out his *"very nude mural"* in the hall, as a concession to middle class taste.) VAST 1st flr. 30ft. drawing rm., nice ceiling, balcony, gd. dining rm., new ground flr. kit. 4/5 bedrms., bathrm., extra kit. for genteel subletting. ONLY £13,990 FHLD.

FASHIONABLE CHELSEA. Fashionable publisher, who has come a long way – via THE NAKED & THE DEAD, since he was employed as a scarecrow in a cherry orchard in '41, now moving to greater affluence, sacrifices small but impressive period style architect blt. ('57) res. Elegant drawing rm., 3 bedrms. The Master bedrm. is big, dble. & superb, the 2nd. O.K. in the 3rd. Mr. Andre Deutsch dares only accommodate the more dwarfish of his less successful writers but, he adds: *"Sunshine & warmth pour in & on a summer eve the street looks like a UTRILLO."* Lux. b. & k. Undeveloped garden. Space for extra rms. &/or GARAGE. Lse. to 1998. G.R. ONLY £45. BARGAIN £8,990

FASHIONABLE DULWICH VILLAGE. White painted family house. Quite a gracious drawing rm. French Windows to garden, now MUSIC RM. *"A piano; no: no tely – I'm lucky I only work on it."* says little EMERGENCY WARD 10 actress who, marrying Film Director must move. Dining rm., study or 5th bedrm., b'fast rm., 4 bedrms., b. & k. Hundreds recently spent. Lse. to 2004. G.R. £8. A gift at £4,550 even try offer.

FLAT BARGAIN. Fleet Air Arm fighter pilot, now, he says, a follower of Bertrand Russell, feels call of sea again (Brighton) and must sacrifice for a purely nominal sum, incl. worthwhile f. & f. this warm and airy 2nd flr. FASHIONABLE LANCASTER GATE FLAT. Impressive 26ft drawing room, 2 bedrms. mod. b & k. CONSTANT HOT WATER. Present lse. 2 years only £525 p.a.

WITH ALL THE THOROUGHNESS OF A TEUTON & NONE OF THE NASTINESS, PAUL HANSARD, the brilliant actor who found it expedient to leave Hitler's Berlin as a child in '34 has superbly modernised this FINE FASHIONABLE ISLINGTON PERIOD HOUSE in wide road of well cared for houses. A most elegant yet comfortable 25ft. double drawing rm. Good dining rm. kit. A study of peace & dignity or 3rd. bedrm. 2 other bedrms. Bathrm. DECOR EXCELLENT. Pleasant small garden, grass & snowdrops. ONLY £8,650 FREEHOLD.

GROUP CAPT. MOVED MUST SHIFT S.E.18 NEW (1961) HOUSE, over 400ft. Panorama, Parliament, The Abbey, St. Paul's, the Thames and the Tower. 15 min. Charing X from BLACKHEATH Stn. where you will rub shoulders with the cream of Suburban Society; surgeons, stockbrokers, chaps on Lloyds. Lawyers or, as an elderly aristocrat described them, his cousin tells me. *"Daily-breaders – dirty b . . . .s"*. SPACIOUS 27ft. drawing rm., decent sized well-fit. kit. "Neighbours can eat in theirs." 3 bedrms., tiled bathrms. Decor v. good. Warm sunny house. Garage, garden. SACRIFICE £4,750, try any offer. Lse. 96 yrs. G.R. £15.

CHEAP FLAT, Sunny side 2nd flr. new ('59) block KINGSTON-ON-THAMES where, by craning the neck, you can see this lovely stretch of river 200 yards away. Stn. (Surbiton) 20 mins. Waterloo. Comfortable drawing rm. with bay window, 2 bedrms., superb 9 ft. fit. wardrobe., mod b & k used as b'fast rm. GARAGE. Use of gdns. Venerable apothecary of the old school will, with his pestle & mortar, pill-making machine & former shorthand typist, be moving next week and we will try any offer on the low fig. of £3,850. Lse 95 yrs. G.R. ONLY £17.

FASHIONABLE CHELSEA, FAMOUS TITE ST., (Where O. Wilde, friend of FRANK HARRIS lived.) Quiet sunny, 3rd. flr. flat off CHEYNE WALK where client, an important theatrical producer of "dustbin" drama and middle class theatre, says he can actually see the river if someone holds his feet. 2 bedrms., elegant drawing rm., altho' in show-biz quiet good taste, no velvet flock wallpaper. A Bolan over fireplace. Mod. tiled bathrm., well fit. b'fast, rm., kit. clkrm., Gd. Lse. 5 yrs. Unrapacious Landlord. ONLY £475 p.a.

G.P.O. FAILED TO RE-OPEN LINE, (closed to foil Feldman's fans) in time for last Sun's ad. Try Again. CHEAP GOOD FLAT of Feldman, the famous tely script writer of ARMY GAME & BOOTSIE & SNUDGE, who somehow achieved success without sadism. PARK WEST sunny 3rd. flr. windows all round. Gorgeous 70ft. swimming pool. Delightful "L" shaped drawing rm. gd. dble. bedrm., mod. bathrm., shower. Well fit. kit. CENT HEAT. C.H.W. Lift. Lse. to March 1965. Only £420 p.a. Low price for f. & f.

BRAVE WOMAN RETURNING S. AFRICA (I warned her that under New edict you can be executed for sticking up an anti-government poster). Sacrifices her newly built, magnificent LUXURY STUDIO FLAT in most fashionable KENSINGTON, W.8 (they won't look at you unless you come from the top social, or, of course, financial brackets). Spacious "L" shaped, under floor heated Oregon pine floor. American kit. Lux. bathrm. Lse. 6 yrs. ONLY £400 p.a. Would flog whole lux. furnishings complete or not.

MR. WISHART (former member, he says, of BAND OF HOPE: & proud descendant of CALVINIST GEO. WISHART who was burnt at the stake at St. Andrews) has given up selling drugs & is going to Edinburgh to sell beer must sell NEW (60) LUX. HOUSE, on the site of ROYAL HUNTING FOREST. Dulwich College grant him access to a bit that's left at the bottom of his garden. ONLY 12 mins. London Bridge. Lovely 1st· flr. drawing rm. & dining rm. to super lab. sav. kit., 3 bedrms., NURSERY or 4th dble. bedrm., lux. bathrm., ONLY £5,550.

ANOTHER OLD CLIENT, EARL RUSSELL seeks house, anywhere LONDON, scruffy area around St. Pancras wld. do. Short lse. abt. 5 yrs. Presumably within that time either sanity or the bomb will have prevailed. With an integrity that is becoming a little old fashioned, the Earl once saw to it that we got our commission on a house when we would not otherwise have done so. Therefore the very least I can say is "No commission required & please try to help".

£4,250 TRY ANY OFFER. Forced to move nearer his lab. & hush-hush work on electronic mousetrap (still on the secret list). B.Sc. of safely negative political opinions sacrifices comfortable & stately mock Tudor (1936) res. half way between Bushey & Richmond Parks (abt. 20 mins. Waterloo). Dble. drawing rm. leads to dining section making a surprisingly fine 30ft. rm. (FINE PARQUET FLR.) leading to rose gdn. & sacred gooseberry bush (strange myths still linger in the suburbs despite my old friend Dr. **st*c* Ch*ss*r). 3 bedrms., mod. tiled bathrm., lab. sav. kit. Enough CENTRAL HEATING. New decor. Long 75 yr. lse. (Fhld. avail. for a trifle).

FELIX FONTEYN, THE FASHIONABLE PHOTOGRAPHER of pre-stressed concrete, beautiful women and Yogi Bear dispensable drinking vessels, offers his smart S. KEN. MEWS COTTAGE WITH GARAGE (1 decent motor or 2 inferior ones), Drawing rm. with dining end, principal double bedrm., with fit. wdrbe. & exotic decor – fabric covered wall & ceiling. A 2nd. bedrm. (it has been found perfectly feasible to keep a child here. This section has been sound proofed), small mod. bathrm, with cork flr. & kit. It is possible to bask on the 25ft. SUN TERRACE. Pres. Lse. 6 yrs. from 2.5.61. ONLY £120 p.a. Try any offer: depends on what you want left.

OCEAN RACER MUST SELL SMART PRINCES GATE MEWS, S.W.7. MEWS COTTAGE with HUGE GARAGE which takes his two cars and more. Charming 1st flr. Drawing rm. Good dble. bedrm., Bathrm., super new kit. Immac. new decor. Living here must be like being pressed between the pages of JENNIFER'S DIARY – the nearest thing to the plebs I have met in the Mews was a charming Hohenzollern Princess who professed Marxism. However, a middle class buyer will probably be tolerantly accepted as *"Someone's chauffeur ..."* Good lease: 10 yrs. extendable/ G.R. ONLY £25. A GIFT AT £5,995.

LUXURY MAYFAIR FLAT which Mrs. P. (a former Archer character who got out just in time before getting her fingers – inter alia – burnt to make a Roman holiday for the B.B.C. who out-horrify the emergent I.T.V.) describes as ravishingly beautiful, aloof (she means there's no lift. R.E.B.) French wallpapers, fabulous Louis XVI marble mantel, real coal fires altho' of course CENTRAL HEATING. Bathroom, an ablutionists dream – solid marble, gold taps to bidet. *"Char might stay...."* Forced move; sacrifice far, far below cost. Elegant drawing rm., 2 fine dble. bedrms, enchanting breakfast rm./kit. Spanish tiles around the double sinks. Lease until March 1977 at £410 p.a. rising in 1966 to £435 p.a. and in 1973 to £460 p.a?

FABULOUS BARGAIN. The Three Shields Gallery off KENSINGTON CHURCH ST. W.8. A dear little GEORGIAN HOUSE converted, in a prosperous shopping street, into thriving gallery (grnd. flr. showrm. & roomy basement, so dry, envelopes stored). 2 offices on 1st flr. or splendid dble. drawing rm. & 3 other gd. rms., b & k. Sells superior mod. pottery (*"nothing art & crafty"*) & the nicer sort of greetings card to an exclusive clientele. (My favourites *"Your face looks as though it's worn out two bodies"* & *"We are at home on Sundays between 5 & 7. Hope you are the same,"* are alas, not in stock.) It's more than a comfortable income – It's a way of life, of course, I suppose there's nothing to stop you turning it into a chop-suey joint, fish parlour or modern art gallery, & really coining the money. A BARGAIN,

NASH MASTERPIECE, PARK VILLAGE WEST. REGENT'S PK. One of the last bastions against Socialism. Describing himself as *"A frustrated young Tory"* (he is only 40 & arranges flowers for a living), our client tires of this lovely house on which he has lavished £4,000 in 2 years. Exquisite 25ft. withdrawing rm., parquet & a fine chimney-piece, elegant dining rm., 2 master bedrms. & marble bathrm. & marble lav., light base. has 2 good bedrms., bathrm. & kit. Top (2nd) flr. has gorgeous 32 × 24 ft. STUDIO, plus good sized model's disrobing rm. Used for Political parties. Crown Lse. 14 yrs. renewable. Only £220 p.a. £8,950.

KEW GARDENS. IMPRESSIVE, GRANDLY MODERNISED, £8–10,000 spent. Impresario & son of a sort of mini-Diaghilev, who claims visitors say his garden is better than KEW (Cumberland Gate opposite). As for the interior it is the perfect exotic for the ballet dancers who flit through the centrally heated entrance hall, large & impressive under the chandelier. Elegant 30ft. "L" drawing rm., fine dining rm., cosy study. 5 DOUBLE bedrms, 12 × 10ft. Dressing rm. or 6th bedrm. 2 lux. bathrms. shower & bidet. Well fit. kit. SUN LOGGIA leading to terrace. GARAGE. ONLY £18,990 FREEHOLD & TRY ANY OFFER.

A REMARKABLE RESIDENT OF THE FASHIONABLE STRAND ON THE GREEN (CHISWICK) instructs us to sell his enchanting rose-clad cottage, snug & dry, garden wall lapped by the tide (OWN PRIVATE MOORINGS). By day the suave Dr. X – by night a powerful, half tamed gorilla-like Actor (one blacked all over as an African slave) fed by his fair wife with flesh at DRACULA BRAM STOKER'S old dining table in the elegant candle lit dining rm. Charming drawing rm. with wonderful river views, super, super kit., 4 bedrms., some murals, brilliant, witty and innocent by 13 yrs. old daughter. Mod. bathrm. shower. Cent. Heat. GARAGE Studio or extra rms. can be built over. Sacrifice £17,995.

ANCIENT 250 YR. OLD WIMBLEDON COMMON COTTAGE: Sweeping views: by 2 golf courses. Elegant drawing rm., bow windows, cosy dining rm., French windows to back yard, 2 dble. bedrms., the lux. bathrm., can only be reached through second bedrm. "No real inconvenience in the case of an attractive blonde guest" says steel wool salesman, now famous cosmetic king. Lavishly modernised & dec. BARGAIN £6,495 FHLD., even try any offer.

CHEAP FLAT, WESTMINSTER, S.W.1. Higher Civil Servant's 4th flr. (No lift) MANSION FLAT (panoramic vista Abbey, Big Ben & that new erection on the Embankment) which, since he was loaned to N.A.T.O. in Paris; he now has 5 children & has now outgrown. Spacious drawing rm., 3 gd. bedrms., bathrm., big kit.-dining rm. (As the lower classes edge away from the kitchen range into separate dining rms. with lit-up cocktail cabinets, their betters are content to breakfast with the Bendix.) Pres. lse. to Jan. '64, said renewable. ONLY £262 p.a. INC. CON. HOT WATER, CENTRAL HEATING & rates. V. mod. fig. inc. f. & f.

WE HAVE BEEN PROMISED ANOTHER EARLY VIC. 6 RM. CHELSEA HOUSE. Whilst not wishing to gloss over its slum-like qualities we ought to mention that our clients will only sell to a person with the taste & means to restore it properly. A foul little garden at the back. ONLY £6,500. Lse. 40 yrs. G.R. abt. £50. In the absence of an enlightened Government which could build better, unsubsidised houses for £2,500, you are unlikely to get anything better.

BUILDING SITE. Worthy Charity has spare lump of land with permissions to erect superior gentleman's res. When, despite sign-posting, you finally motor up out of the hell that is S.E. London, It's nice to see the green verges &, perched up here in BICKLEY, surrounded by wooded hills, it's odd that you're only 25 mins. from town by train. We don't, of course, charge commission for this sort of job, so you'll get it net. – ROY BROOKS.

NO HOUSE yet in response to last week's appeal for scruffy house, pref. near Waterloo, a crude shelter for derelict female tramps who must still drag their tired sick frames from one disturbed place of rest (sic) to another. A reader from Wales writes offering to give a tenth of his income to this project. His income is £4.11.0 a week! It's a pity that our society which can still spew out millions on palaces & Ascot grandstands cannot succour those whose aggressive & acquisitive instincts – or less fortunate birth – ill-equip them to compete in our affluent society. **ROY BROOKS.**

GENTEEL NEW MALDEN, abt. 15 mins. Waterloo. SECLUDED IN A GORGEOUS GARDEN (We are told about ¾ acre) surrounded by trees solidly fits the stately suburban house of proprietor of Teenage Twisting Club in the heart of Soho. Spacious lounge/hall, 3 recep. rms., 5/6 bedrms., 2 bathrms., gd. kit., large studio. 2 garages. Just call Sunday after 10 a.m. Thetford Road. £10,500 FREEHOLD.

LAWN CRES. KEW. Oddly enough it really does overlook a lawn, surrounded by trees which obscure view of Pagoda. RICHMOND PARK is over the hill. Former A.D.C. Governor of Tanganyika MUST SELL solid family res. Spacious drawing rm., in fashionable mud-green the whole place in House & Garden colours, dining rm. to garden which has been exposed to the ravages of 5 children. Super Kit. AGA, 5 bedrms., splendid balcony, mod. bathrm. £6,500.

LIFE AT THE TOP OF PUTNEY HILL o'looking HEATH. In well tended grounds; the mode. LUX. BLOCK 1st. flr. FLAT of *"Socialist miner's son from the Welsh Valleys"* who has made good in Advertising. *"At Oxford got a 1st. in History – it helps – the logic y'know – promoted pink toilet soap on tely, filmed nude French model in her bath ..."* Ent. hall, drawing rm. PARQUET & door to balcony. 3 Bedrm., bathrm., well fit. kit. GARAGE. Lse. 93 yrs. GR ONLY £40. SACRIFICE £6,995.

WELSH MAIDEN, descended from King Edward III & an old friend of His Majesty, makes the supreme sacrifice, & sadly parts with her MOD. LUX. BLOCK SUNNY 2nd flr. FLAT & all f. & f. – save the family sword for a mod fig. Drawing rm. with sunbathing balcony, double bedrm., mod b. & k. *"The decor's pretty awful but there's CENTRAL HEATING c.h.w., lift,"* & she says, *"The nicest porters. . . ."* Lse. 3 yrs. Only £315 p.a.

CHELSEA IS FASHIONABLE, that is why it attracts predatory business men, with their awful wives & poorer envious detractors. All being slowly poisoned by the filthy effluvia of Lots Road Power Station, the Gas Works & a strong whiff from Battersea Power Station (it was only when they found that its corrosive fumes were attacking the fabric of London's ancient buildings that they did a partial filtration). One of my friends in this road (Limerston St.) a successful but still happy architect, loves the place. *"On Saturday afternoon,"* he says, *"I take a bus to Peter Jones & stroll back looking at the shops, the pretty girls . . ."*. This horror has 8 rooms, 2 thrown into one rm. about 32ft., with chimney-piece blood red painted marble & leprous yellow tiles, old shallow sink & coal fuel copper. The coal seems, recently, to have been removed from the bath itself. Upstairs the decor is fairly new, clean and in execrable taste. The oilcloth strikes a jarring note throughout. A small patch of earth behind. Lse. abt. 40 yrs. G.R. £60. ONLY £6,850. KEY OFFICE but tread with caution on the rotten basement boards.

£3,500 FREEHOLD. The airy, elegant SPAN HOUSE of England's Design Consultant of sanitary ware, lampposts & other modern conveniences: forced out by fecundity. The LARGE L-shaped double reception rm., 3 bedrms., mod. bathrm., kit. Garden with squirrel & GARAGE. TWICKENHAM, in the bucolic environs of RICHMOND OLD DEER & BUSHEY PARKS, yet quick to Piccadilly. Owner eschewing Sabbatical pistol practice will show today.

1ST. FLOOR SUNNY SOUTH FLAT. KENSINGTON PARK GARDENS. Overlooking & access to 7 acres of private gardens. The magnificent home of lady opera singer & former agricultural worker. The impressive & gorgeously comfortable 22ft. × 20ft. drawing rm., with sun bathing balcony, HUGE 20ft. double bedrm. with sort of Romeo & Juliet balcony, mod. b. & k. The decor strikes a high note. Lse. 5 yrs. from last quarter. ONLY £340 p.a. This impulsive couple will probably accept a miserably low fig. for f. & f. from a deserving case.

£990 FASHIONABLE CHELSEA. A dreadful working-class terrace house of sinister aspect in one of the meaner streets at the bitter end of CHEYNE WALK in the grimy ambit of LOTS RD. POWER STN. Time and decay have not softened the hideous aspect of this typical example of Victorian speculative building. 6 rms., kit. (generations of women have looked out, over the shallow sink with its one cold tap, slap onto the crumbling, claustrophobic backyard and outside lav.). The Master bedrm. has had its door torn off at the hinges, several windows have been broken, what is left of the paintwork is in a nasty, dirty shade of green and the wallpaper hangs dankly down in shreds – otherwise there's probably not much wrong, as people have been living in it up to now. The gaping holes gnawed at the edges in the basement flr. may not have been done by rats, but merely large mice. Lse. 17 yrs. G.R. abt. £10. View Sun. The door swings open in the wind: Stadium Street, S.W.10.

FASHIONABLE KNIGHTSBRIDGE. Rich electrician bought this period res. to extend his gracious living next door, has cut off this 1st flr. FLAT with own street door & has lavishly reconstructed it to the same standards as his own & to tell the truth, not in bad taste. Simply crawling with electric plugs. Attractive drawing rm., gd. dble. bedrm., luxury bath-dressing rm. with shower. Gd. well fit. kit. big enough to eat in. Lse. 12 yrs. ONLY £100 p.a. £5,750, but a lower price wedded to a higher rent cld. be arranged to marry in with a buyer's expense account. After all there is something rather sacred about the preservation of money over other merely material considerations.

ONLY £285 p.a., excl. MOD. BLOCK. V. Sunny 3rd flr. FLAT, Eaton Rise, N.W.2. Beautiful views thro' trees to distant slaughterhouse. CND Lady Drama Instructor – husband is in a museum – lavished money: now bought house & sacrifices 21 yrs. lse. Delightful drawingrm., dble. bedrm., mod. bathrm., well fit. kit. Lift, Porters, C.H. V. mod. fig. to inc. f. & f.

BUCOLIC ESHER. Bearded advertising art director and inventor of patent plastic process for preserving poissons for pub walls and posterity must sell splendid new Architect-built (1960) det. res., surrounded by farmland. Gorgeous L-shaped 28ft × 21ft. drawing rm., small study, 4 bedrms., tiled lux. bathrm. SUPERBLY FIT. KIT. DBLE. STAINLESS SINK. OIL FIRED CENTRAL HEATING. GARAGE. EASY GARDEN, PEACE AND PRIVACY FOR ONLY £8,950 FHLD. (A bargain; the newly enriched lower middle classes pay up to £20,000 to be herded together in those ghastly Estates.)

LABOUR SAVING CASTLE: The lucky buyer of this erection dailybreading on the 7.49 (under an hour to Charing X) with R*v**ll* tucked in the Times knows that with *"Castle"* on his writing paper & a building 175ft high nobody can look down on him any longer. And all for the price of a suburban Villa – £4,995 FREEHOLD. Some gorgeous reception rooms 30ft high. As to bedrooms, it depends how high you want to climb. No bath, of course. Mains electricity, gas & water available. Well built & must have cost the earth even in 1810.

FASHIONABLE BLACKHEATH, SUPER SUNNY STH. ASPECT SPAN FLAT. 1st (top) flr. set in lovely woodland glade sort of gdns. with safe children's playgrnd. decently removed. Congenial professional neighbours who carry their economic serfdom lightly, altho' cut to the quick when a local P.C. referred to "Those Council flats at the Priory." Charming well proportioned drawing rm., with dining annexe, 3 bedrms., tiled bathrm., super kit., bar with high stools. Delightful decor chosen by Cordon Bleu painter bride.

FASHIONABLE   ISLINGTON. A
vaguely ecclesiastical atmosphere broods
over   this   scheduled-for-preservation
GOTHIC REVIVAL GARDEN SQUARE.
(I know Estate Agents have debased the
meaning of *"Unique"* but our Mr. Halstead
says it really is). In this 12 rm. res. of English
speaking Australian Surgeon, 2 in the base.
are rather sordid & top is attic but the rest
are not bad if you discount the decor which
is dirty, dark & depressing. Not entirely without plumbing, there is a cold tap around
somewhere. Garden, heavily disguised under
a patch of weeds. Client says house has a
good survey. GREAT BARGAIN £7,850
FHLD. & try any, yes ANY OFFER.

BUSINESS WE DON'T WANT. Houses outside London & client's who rat by using a good offer they have accepted to tempt another buyer to overbid; breaking their word & soiling our national reputation. **PLEASE DON'T MAKE OUR LIFE MORE DIFFICULT** by instructing us if you are not **A MAN OR WOMAN OF YOUR WORD.** I am getting more than a little tired of people, of apparently good standing, who accept a good offer and then *"rat"* for a pathetically few *"pieces of silver"*. I pose a question to the men which does work 7 times out of 10; but I have yet to find an epithet that one can use to a woman. My apologies to country clients & my pity for the rats – after all there is no one more difficult to get away from than yourself. **ROY BROOKS.**

RED BEARDED ARCHITECT forced thro' enormous growth of family, to emigrate to Ealing. **MUST SELL** cherished Period rws. off **HOLLAND PARK AVE.** Graceful 27ft. dble. drawing rm., 5 single bedrms. (2 cld. be converted to dble. in case anyone wanted to sleep together). Boxrm., mod. bathrm. Big dining rm.-kit. The decor? – parts of it are excellent. Good garden. **BARGAIN: £6,500 FHLD.** (A Fhld. in Kensington at under £10,000 is becoming a rarity.)

£4,995 FREEHOLD. WELL KNOWN ACTOR R*B*RT BR*CKM*N speaking from his London home of his Liverpool Premiers – & the music teacher in C. P. SNOW'S The Affair, informs us that, after his sojourn at **THE MERMAID** has decided to divide his time between his 3-acre farm in Suffolk : a pied-a-terre (he is now distributing Playboy Magazine) – thereby relinquishing this **TOWN RES.** – best part of **BATTERSEA** – nearer the Park than the Gas Works. A Nolan Henry Moore & Modigliani embellish the pine pannelling of the 25ft. split-level drawing rm., bedrm accom. comprises: The master's bedrm., a nursery & the ex-au-pair girl's room. mod. bathrm., American kit. by Heals. Cheerfully crawling with children, there is no immaculate conception and the gdn. is a patch of flattened earth – but what on earth do you expect for the price?

*NTH*NY BL*ND'S FASHIONABLE ISLINGTON LUX. LOWER MAIS FOR THE UPPER (FINANCIAL) CLASSES. Acclaimed by National Press who, by happy coincidence, all happened to drop in the other week. Plumbed in alcohol flushes out of a fountain. Level with garden which plunges down into the rustic canal, bounded by noble, ancient trees, is the GRAND 30ft. super, super DRAWING RM. & split-level Dining area. Super fit. kit. 3 bedrms. & rm. for 4th. 3 lux. bathrms. The illusion of looking out onto the 18th Century from central heated luxury. If you only have the cash this place will give you the cachet.90 yrs. lse. G.R. £125 SACRIFICE £28,750.

ADAM & EVE MEWS, KENSINGTON, W.8. 1st. flr. FLAT. Luxuriously appointed home of Ballet Dancer & *"Toy Barrister with a socialist conscience. Absolutely ideal for a Bachelor,"* he adds, *"'or anyone else who has lots of money & lots of personality ..."* Wide, pine panelled Hall & staircase, delightful 22ft. Drawing rm., recess bar & bookshelves. Small dining'rm. to PATIO SUNBATHING ROOF GARDEN. Smashing dble. bedrm. Lux. bathrm., BIDET, PLATE GLASS DOOR TO SHOWER. Super mod. kit. ONLY £50 p.a. Lse. 8¼ yrs. SACRIFICE £4,950. "I might" he says, "sell my fab. furniture & my country cottage – in Beds. – cheap."

DARKEST PIMLICO. A large Victorian family house, entrance flanked by pillars, pathetically waits for purchaser. The bath shrouded by thickening dust. Torn up by its roots the missing geyser leaves a gaping hole. On the Grnd. flr., folding doors open to 27ft. dble. recep. room or shut to make 2 rooms. Folding doors to 1st flr. make L reep. rm. abt. 27ft. × 18ft. A bedrm. & bathrm. 2nd. flr. 3 more bedrms. Groping in the basement, 3 rooms, our intrepid representative stumbled against an ancient brick copper: presumably the kitchen. Long 80 yrs. lse. G.R. £60 p.a. A gift at £6,990. If you are too late to secure this gem we have a twin (a much lighter house equally repulsive) next door in Sutherland Street coming on the market this week at the same price.

BARGAIN. FASHIONABLE CHELSEA SQUARE. Spacious semi-detached family period res. now too big for gentleman engineer whose family have left home (in a '29 Alvis, front wheel drive & elderly Rolls – thus releasing valuable parking space outside). Possible, he says, to build penthouse/studio on top. 6 bedrms., fine 31ft. 1st flr. drawing rm., balcony, dining rm., large study, 2 bathrms., plus excellent basement with own bathrm, Garden & possible garage space. All a trifle scruffy, of course, but what on earth do you expect for £23,550 FHLD.

LITTLE VENICE. Not only fashionable but, judging by the neighbours, a veritable compost heap of culture. Sunny 1st flr. mais. overlkg. beautiful gardens; haunt of wild birds. Gracious 24ft. × 18ft. drawing rm., big 18 × 18ft. dining rm., 3 best bedrms., attic for servant &/or Master's study, b. & k. Lse. 9 yrs. ONLY £450 p.a.

FASHIONABLE LENNOX GARDENS, CHELSEA. Retired Naval Officer, self-styled broiler king and architect sacrifices lower ground floor flat. Dble. drawing rm., dble. bedrm., mod. b. & k. Well fitted – decent taste, which is more than he claimed for his fowls ("Never eat 'em.") V. modest fig. to include f. & f. Use Garden Sq. Lse. 2 yrs. ONLY £350 p.a.

HYDE PARK GATE – *"best address in London,"* says Advert Tycoon sweltering in his shirt sleeves & braces in the full blast of the super CENTRAL HEATING of splendid Mansion Flat decorated with the consummate taste he has displayed in promoting *"silk stockings, cosmetics & lux twin toilet tissue."* Lounge hall, noble 25ft drawing rm., 22ft dining rm., spacious kitchen, mod. sink etc., 3 splendid bedrooms, basins in 2 and fitted wardrobes, boxroom, mod. bathrm. Gleaming wood floors. Lse 5 yrs. at ONLY £450 p.a. £2,850 (to include valuable f. & f.)

KNIGHTSBRIDGE BARGAIN. The gracious ent. flr. MAISONETTE in exclusive GARDEN SQ. (access). Luxuriously dec. in a rather Frenchy manner by avant garde French actor who, turning from the plays of J. P. Sartre to plumbing, is now retiring to S. of France & must dispose, albeit, at far, far below cost. Spacious & lovely drawing rm., pale violet carpeted dining rm. or 3rd bedrm., 2 other bedrms., close carpeted bathrm., mod. kit. Costly velvet flock wallpapers. The gdn. in due season a bower of roses, fig & sycamore, looks awful at pres. Lse. $2\frac{3}{4}$ yrs. ONLY £375 p.a. (Or new 5-yr. lse. £500 p.a.)

DOLCE VITA IN EALING. MODERN LUXURY FLAT BLOCK. A sort of hive for drones egged on by the facilities – swimming, billiards, fun & games – the pampered tenants live Eloi-like in between flitting to the executive suites. Wearing nothing (but their dark business suit, grammar school tie & bowler), tenants lie soaking up the sun on the communal lawn. Cosy drawing rm. to balcony. Dining rm./3rd. bedrm. 2 bedrms., k. & b. Lse. 3 yrs. Rent £385 p.a.

FASHIONABLE PIMLICO. Early VICTORIAN TOWN HOUSE of 9 rms., 3 with pretty grim baths stuck in corner. Decorative defects include a fine growth of fungus on the wall of ground floor rear room. The first floor 27ft. drawing rm. is marred by the marble mantlepiece which has left its moorings and is sprawled across the floor. A fussy purchaser would presumably have the gaping hole in the top bedrm. ceiling – open to the sky – repaired. Lse. 80 yrs. G.R. £70. ONLY £8,650.

£5,775 FREEHOLD TRY ANY OFFER. *"Go to Brooks, I was told by a client of yours, who said you got her £1,000 more than she expected,"* said the High Pressure (CO2) Beverage Advertising Chief. *"But as I've bought another I'll take low price for immediate sale."* Nr. STREATHAM COMMON superbly blt. just pre 1st German War but looks later, early Tudor revival, all very cosy with beamed drawing rm. with bkshelves & display cabinet & racks for the Famille Vert. *"Keatsean"* leaded light casements, beamed lounge hall with fire and seat, Gd. dining rm., kit. plus b'fast rm., 3 bedrms., bathrm., Decent gdn. with fishpond. You might take the garage where he kept his vintage Bugattis, only 11/- p.w.

£2,675. Lse. to 2012. G.R. ONLY £9.10. London Editor & girl sur-tax examiner's modernised Period Cottage: Choumert Sq., an oasis of gentility in S.E.15 – 6 mins. London Bridge, an Hon. among the neighbours & easy reach Dulwich & other parks. Forced move; she needs more space for her children & he wants bigger kt. & Aga for his compost bread-making. Cosy drawing rm., 2 gd. bedrms.. mod. b. & k. Decor in decent taste but homely rather than the sort of place where they eat their cigarette ends has almost survived the onslaughts of their children. Play forecourt which some turn to garden.

MEWS COTTAGE OFF PARK LANE, by the DORCHESTER. 2 GARAGES. 1ST Flr. flat: attractive drawing rm., dble. bedrm., mod. b. & k. Vac. poss. or top lets for £8 p.w. & 1st. flr. for £25–35 p.w. GARAGES at £9 10s. Lse. 10 yrs. from last Sep. ONLY £800 p.a. £3,990 try ANY, yes ANY offer as our client, a notable horsewoman, is champing at the bit.

FASHIONABLE BLACKHEATH PARK. The Lane. One of the better SPAN HOUSES: end of only three, rural setting o'er preserved open land. Really splendid 25ft. drawing rm. floor to ceiling picture windows. Study, super fit. kit./b'fast rm., 3 bedrms., lux. bathrm., patio & walled gdn. GARAGE. Anthropologist, having completed his studies on the Span Man is going to Scotland to study Pictish Burials, leaves his OPUNTIA GIGANTICARIX (you wouldn't get this monster housebound 7ft. cactus out without a fight anyway). BARGAIN £7,990. Lse. 97 yrs. G.R. £30 p.a.

£2,450 FREEHOLD. PIERS HAGGARD sacrifices humble cottage 'twixt Battersea Pk. & Clapham Common as, after working on Beckett, Rookery Nook, Genet's The Blacks and other Masters of modern drama, he has turned his back on London (*"Blast"* said one of his great uncle's heroes; *"the first time he had used strong language in front of a lady."* – I wonder what he would have made of Genet?) Drawing rm., 2 bedrms., mod. b. & k. Garden: a small wilderness.

FASHIONABLE DULWICH *"A village of 2,000 Squires"* says Fred M. the well known Operatic Conductor *"you see 'em in the pub airing their ambitions, their pretty young wives left at home – it's known as the adultery belt ...."* A spacious family house, sunny & fairly soundproof *"We've had the Berlin Ensemble in the 1st flr. Music rm. & none of the neighbours complained."* Comfortable 20ft. Drawing rm. Gd. dining rm. Kit. Study or 5th bedrm., 4 other bedrms. (1 as extra nursery, kit. or genteel sublet). Mod. bathrm. Garden, apple tree & number of neglected plants. £6,490 FREEHOLD.

DOLCE VITA IN HISTORIC HOUNSLOW, on the very ground worked by DICK TURPIN, important TELEVISION MAN (It's frightfully convenient for all the T.V. Studios) has created, in reality, the idealised gracious living seen in his commercials – Scandinavian woodwork & all that. A NEW ('63) end-of-ter. TOWN HOUSE with private landscaped garden (he's erected 6ft. high fences, willow, apple, pear & peach trees lawn & profusion of flowers. Fast tube etc. town. Smashing 25ft. dble. drawing rm. dining area, superfit kit. Wrighton units. 2 DBLE. Bedrms, fit. wdrbs., lux. tiled bathrm. Cedar & glass sunrm., to patio & gdn. FULL CENT. HEATING. GARAGE PLUS CARPORT. It's a bottle of Beaujolais with the steaklets & two cars if you want to count in Hounslow Society today. ONLY £6,475

£5,975 FREEHOLD – try any offer. OFF SOUTHSIDE, CLAPHAM COMMON. With art nouveau raising its sinister sinuous head, this fin de siècle erection should command respect. This all too solidly built family house spacious 25ft. dble drawing rm., b'fast rm. to garden (3 apple trees) 5 bedrms., bathrm. & kit.

£5,950! THE BWANA OF BLACK-HEATH, returning from E. African Diamond Mines, has staked a claim to the SPAN HOUSE with the LARGEST Triple-sized garden. Spacious 'L' Drawing rm., a wall of plate glass to Wistaria clad patio & garden, well fit. kit., 3 bedrms., mod. bathrm. The whole place bristles with beautiful black busts which seduces the eye from the less than perfect decor, due to subletting when in Africa: anyway it's a TERRIFIC BARGAIN. Lse. 991 yrs. G.R. £20.

CHOKING with what an old friend of mine, who helped to invent smokeless district heating, called *"Aerial Sewerage"* many of our applicants are too debilitated to face a long journey and prefer to grope around the centre where we URGENTLY NEED HOUSES FOR SALE (I can't imagine anyone in their right mind wanting to live in London) ROY BROOKS.

FASHIONABLE CHELSEA S.W.3. Barrister & Labour candidate moving further away from his Constituency MUST SELL his NON BASE reconstructed Period House. GLEAMING NEW WHITE DECOR. 25ft. dble. drawing rm., leading to rm. for kit. (anyone eating or washing up at home wld. install sink). 4 bedrms. could get dble. bed in all. He's had all the breasts removed & CENT. HEAT RADIATORS installed throughout. He wouldn't be drawn on Labour Policy on VIETNAM but ended on an optimistic note. "The sun" he said "shines all the time on my secluded sunbathing roof garden..." ONLY £11,995 FREEHOLD

YOUNG MRS. DOUCH THE DOCTOR'S WIFE (*"I'm frequently taken for the au pair girl"*) enthusiastically recommends her cheerful, superbly modernised Victorian EALING FAMILY HOUSE to anyone like herself with 5 children under 6½. Lovely ground floor nursery with own bathrm. Magnificent 25ft. family dining rm.-kit. AGA. Quiet comfortable withdrawing rm. 1st flr. 3 dble. & 1 single bedrm. Mod. bathrm. 2nd. flr. more bedrms. & kitchenette. Decor as reasonable as you could expect with 5 happy children. LARGE GARDEN. GARAGE. A GIFT AT £10,995 FREEHOLD.

WILL NO ONE BUY THIS POOR OLD HOUSE? Empty, miserable & racked by the District trains that pass at the end of its tiny, overgrown & possibly in very good shape back gdn. Now arranged as VACANT SPACIOUS S/c MAISONNETTES. Enormously rich owner is not really interested in money as long as we find someone sympathetic for this BARON'S COURT gem. He is only asking £8,250 FREEHOLD.

N∗CH∗L∗S T∗M∗L∗N, Editor of TOWN & President of the Society for the discouragement of Public Relations, modestly describes his FASHIONABLE GREENWICH WM. & Mary house & decor as: *"Gorgeous, superb, lavish ..... the magnificent new CENTRAL HEATING enables the fireplaces to be converted to hi-fi .... Most splendid large drawing rm. French windows to the garden of 100 ripening peaches, figs which arrive at comparative maturity & vine heavy with the sweetening grape, apples & lawn for baby croquet."* The dining rm. is not bad either. *"Fabulous kit."* Vast prowling study or playroom of *"Athletic"* proportions (33½ft), 4 principal bedrms., mod. bathrm., PLUS top FLAT 2 gd. rms., own b. & k. N.T. thinks would suit rich young couple over span of their childbearing in healthy verdant surroundings. 9 mins. London Bridge. Lse. 14 yrs. ONLY £600 p.a. SACRIFICE £6,995. Permitted genteel subletting cld. reduce total liability to £300 p.a. Might sell FREEHOLD.

GIRL COWBOY EDITRESS & PRO'S FASHIONABLE BARNES WHITE PERIOD COTTAGE. A bucolic life – swimming in the river, 2 mins. away & romping on common – all a few mins. W. End by car (in the middle of the night) 25ft. open plan drawing rm., library, whole wall of super pine bookshelves. 2 bedrms., mod. bathrm., well fit. kit. Decor good. Garden SACRIFICE £6,275 FHLD.

POSH KINGSTON HILL, graced by many famous & illustrious people, H.M. Queen Victoria hunted the stags & H.M. King Farouk spent part of his boyhood here. A perfectly splendid 2nd (top) flr. FLAT: gorgeous panorama over Richmond Park, directly behind. Converted mansion, but MAGNIFICENT 25ft. Scandinavian style DRAWING RM. (6 big windows) newly built on. 3 bedrms. mod. bathrm., new kit. Dec. in exquisite taste by Grammar School anti-Monarchical Conservative Avant garde Architect, who must flog it quick. GARAGE inc. Use ¼ acre Garden. Sacrifice £4,750 try any offer. Lse. 97 yrs., G.R. ONLY £25.

10 PEOPLE WANTED LAST WEEK'S KENTISH TOWN HOUSE, one of the disappointed nine left the office in tears. RE-PLACEMENTS URGENTLY WANTED, however scruffy, as long as it's under £10,000. (We still have plenty of demand for decent £20,000 houses, but these applicants keep more cheerful). Usual scale commission. ROY BROOKS.

APOLOGIES TO THOSE EARLY CALLERS who failed to contact Client who failed to tell Hotel operator: now frantic has slashed price £1,000. THAMES DIT-TON. Smell of country, 30 mins. Waterloo. Another of that ambient Monarch Henry VIIIth's Hunting Lodges where, it is said, he kept a mistress. (Live in a suburb where everyone knows your business). Refaced, probably in Queen Anne's time. Vast sums spent. Charming drawing rm., gd. dining rm., utility rm., 3 best bedrms. plus bedsit for dwarf. mod. b. & k. Historically named ROSEWOOD HOUSE. The lovely gdn. breeds a gorgeous profusion of roses, peaches and gooseberries. DOUBLE GARAGE. Sacrifice £5,990 FHLD. A det. modernised staff cottage: 3 rms. new b. & k. ONLY £3,550.

£6,500 FREEHOLD. MISS WHITTING-TON & HER CAT (The long-tailed Barge variety which swims) offer their family home, since 1910. A fine solid Victorian family home. Ent. hall, a rather nice staircase with sweeping curved bannister, down which this charming scion of an ancient lineage used to slide *"girls of my generation were silly until they were forty .... we used to have a gover-ness, cook, between maid & under-maid & a weekly washerwoman. MILLER the butcher's sheep grazed on the nearby common, BAD-COCK the Postmaster-General lived in the middle of the road where he had the pillar box erected outside his gate."* The road only really began to go down when LLOYD GEORGE came to live in it. Comfortable drawing rm., dining rm., drs, to garden, b'fastrm. leading to kit., 5 bedrms. (4 DOUBLE), period bathrm., admirable store rms. & wine cellar. 90 ft. garden.

THE FASHIONABLE BLACKHEATH GEORGIAN TEA-CADDY HOUSE of Dr. X, a successful Arborfield apprentice now in rubber goods and French mistress (secondary mod.) Detached dble. fronted. 30ft. dble. drawing rm. fine large Dining rm. leading to well fit. kit. 6 bedrms., 4 dble., bathrm. PLUS s/c semi-basement flat of 2 large rooms b. & k. Gorgeous big garden onto playing fields. £15,750 FREEHOLD.

FASHIONABLE CHELSEA. A clapped out EARLY VICTORIAN VILLA. Semi-detached so you can get your motorbike round to the dirty patch of weeds which passes for a garden. 27ft. double drawing rm., Dining rm. & dreadful basement kit. 3 bedrms. & room for a bathrm. if desired. Dirty, dark brown varnished woodwork dating back to the General Strike: Peeling wallpaper & plaster work (need redecorating). Look out for "Merulious Lacrymans." Quiet backwater abutting hospital laundry. Lse. 51 yrs. G.R. £80 p.a. Bargain £8,950.

PERRY GUINESS IS GOOD FOR YOU. Unable to face another 22 yrs. of well paid (for the B.B.C.) security with the Corps., he is emigrating to Australia & MUST QUICKLY SELL all that taste, money & great comfort can provide in the shape of this exceptional REGENCY HOUSE o'er the canal in FASHIONABLE ISLINGTON. Entirely sep., s/c base. flat let to impeccable air pilot 12 gns. p.w. (but poss. if req.) Ent. Hall, clkrm., the casual elegance of a genuine upper-class drawing rm. (25ft.) 3 dble bedrms., fit. wdrbs., mod. bathr., even a rail to warm the towels. Well fit. kit., stainless unit. CENTRAL HEATING, electric NOT Gas which after 160 yrs. of public supply still has its teething troubles. Decor, of course, excellent. £13,995 FREEHOLD.

CHEAP MAIS. WIMBLEDON PARK ROAD. S.W. 18. 3 bedrms., drawing rm., kit.-dining rm., large bathrm. Sunny 1st & 2nd flrs. Not fearfully attractive. *"The best advice I can give on this property,"* says eminent surveyor, *"is demolition."* But what on earth can one expect for £2,995? 99 yr. lse. at only £15 G.R.

SOCIAL OUTCASTS REQUIRE ACCOMMODATION. A modest proposal. Christian Action asks us to find cheap, scruffy houses for homeless, hopeless derelict women near Railway Termini where, constantly moved on, they desperately try to sleep. No hymns or attempts to convert them to merits of Christian Capitalism, just temporary shelter, tea & bread. No *"administration expenses"* the pleasant young women run it for love. Please help: I'm less afraid of do-gooders than those who do damn all. ROY BROOKS.

COMING UP CAMBERWELL. Hid, Casbah-like behind a black door in a high wall in LOVE WALK is the SUPER MOD. DETACHED HOUSE blt. 4 yrs. ago by a brace of young ARCHITECTS (she beautified the new City of London Public Cleansing Depot). Now with 4 babies they've had to build a larger erection & MUST SELL this one sequestered in charming walled garden. with ancient mulberry tree. Ent. Hall, TEAK PARQUET, really lovely 24ft drawing rm., MAPLE Flr., DBLE GLAZING, Westmoreland slate hearth, serving unit, dining rm. or 4th bedrm., 3 bedrms., DEEP fit. wdrbs. fit. basin, mod. bathrm., ONLY £9,450 FREEHOLD.

FASHIONABLE CHELSEA, A PRETTY LOW PERIOD HOUSE (3 floors only). Basement: 3 rms. one with shower. Grnd. flr: decent enough 25ft. dble. rm., windows both ends, another rm., study or 4th bedrm., 1st flr: 3 rooms & space for bathrm. for anyone wanting this rather bourgeois appurtenance. Decor a trifle Bohemian. Bare walls are papered with newspapers from Eastern Europe, prints, childish graffiti. Banisters are missing since I last saw the house – but then, it was a cold winter ... Force your way thru' thick undergrowth, in the tiny garden, and you come to a fig tree. Lse. 40 yrs. G.R. only £60 p.a. Bargain £6,990. Done up they make well over £10,000.

LADY X, former showgirl, now mistress of a couple of mansions & *"a thousand shaggy beasts"* casually casts aside what she describes as: *"Rather scruffy flat over greengrocers in Westbourne Grove ..."* 1st flr. 2 bedrms. sit. rm., mod. bathrm., decently fit. kit. *"Cker, Frg. & drying Cbnet just paid for."* Pres. lse. to July '67. ONLY £382 rising to £436 p.a. SACRIFICE £3,950.

A "LADY" IN OLD PUNCH DRAWING SAID *"Although I live in Balham I feel I spiritually belong in West Kensington"* de Gustibus – anyway this large Red Brick Victorian Perham Road W.14 house has been modernised and has some very decent rooms. 1st. flr. drawing rm. to balcony, dining rm., door to garden. 3 bedrms., dressing rm. or 4th bedrm., bathrm., well fit. kit. Small garden. Lse. 122 yrs. £9,990.

IT'S THE PEOPLE NOT THE PROPERTIES who make life interesting. In '63 little blond actress & singer, Bloomsbury born, blue eyed beauty from the Israeli army (as bright as her great-uncle who collaborated with Curé) but *"had some bother with my bomb throwing – who hasn't ...."* came to see me for a flat. This week, on the sleeve of her hauntingly beautiful LP "AVIVA" BENNY GREEN writes *"ROY BROOKS who is as ruthless in his assessment of women as he is of houses,"* says "if she was a house I could sell her at once ... like a Marx brother only better looking." If you missed her singing on television ask for the disc. No commission required. ROY BROOKS.

FASHIONABLE GREENWICH quiet backwater CROOMS HILL GROVE almost Regency Cottage. Huge Public Work Contractor reconstructed it in a masterly fashion for own occupation – today these chaps are middle class, ties instead of chokers. The decoration is in impeccable taste. Delightful open plan drawing rm., dining rm., with chatelaine space heater leading to well fit. kit. 2 dble. bedrms., lux. bathrm., sunny paved garden. FREEHOLD £8,995.

OFF FASHIONABLE HOLLAND PK. AVE. The beautifully dec. Period home of Lady Potter & gifted Designer. *"Labour: but socialist, of course, rather than Gaitskell ...'* An admirable drawing rm., new grnd. flr. kit. 4 bedrms., mod. bathrm, plus abysmal basement. Ideal for anyone wanting to keep a couple of house servants: or plans to convert to a rich investment. £6,550 FHLD.

IT USED TO BE SAID that you can judge a man by his car: but where you live is probably a better index: & what better address than S. EATON Pl., BELGRAVIA? Here, for the ridiculously low price of £2,995 you can get a theatrical tycoon's lush maisonnette with magnificent 24ft. × 18ft. drawing rm., exotic dining kit., 2 gd. dble. bedrms., mod. bathrm. & suddenly, you come across the sort of panelled discreetly-lit cocktail bar you'd find hidden in a Moscow hotel. Prs. Lse. to '75 ONLY £300 p.a.

CRI DE COEUR: *"Do you ever help impecunious but hard working young people?"* writes quiet educated girl from *"A rather unpleasant bed-sitter for which I am paying an extortionate rent .... tried sharing flat – final straw: one of the other girls abandoned latest boyfriend in my bed & row blew up when I asked him to spend rest of night on settee ...."* She is prepared to give services, cleaning etc. in return for something civilised at reasonable rent. Please help. ROY BROOKS.

WELL DECORATED POET & SOLDIER (D.S.O. & 2 Bars &c.) and alleged female spy offer their desirable family residence off PUTNEY HILL as they are going to live in a kiln. Drawingrm. drs. to rather lovely garden, well stocked with fruits & lilies of the valley. Big study, somewhat gloomy dining rm., big warm bathrm., kit., 5 bedrms. GIFT AT £5,990 FREEHOLD.

AN AIR OF GENTEEL DECAY hangs over this Nash masterpiece in Kent Terrace, REGENT'S PARK. Town residence of son of famous film star, young Dr. X, The Psychiatrist, who dismisses it with refreshing candour, rare in a vendor, *"a dull house with 3 lousy bathrooms, ... a few miserable lilies-of-the-valley in the tiny back garden, we found the dachshund carrying bone – a humerus; but we never found the rest ..."* The usual imposing 1st flr. "L" drawing rm. ample dining rm., study, abt 5 bedrms & a couple of kits. Roof for sunbathing. £300 p.a. to Oct. 63 then 21 years at ONLY £485 p.a. SACRIFICE £5,550 EVEN TRY OFFER.

BENEFICENT BROMLEY. Flat Bargain. High amongst the tree tops, the top (2nd flr.) Eyrie of Man from the Pru & little Milliner; enjoying the panoramic vista across London from this large detached edifice (circa 1900) – more reminiscent of Chas. Addams than Robert Adam. Clkrm., spacious drawing rm., 2 dble. bedrooms (one 24ft.), mod. bathrm., large kit., good decor – gleaming white paintwork. Own garden & Carriage drive for car (ritualistic Sunday morning public ablutions of the Jag. is a common form of worship in the suburbs). Lse. 984 yrs. G.R. £9 p.a. ONLY £3,750.

£4,950. Winglet of WM. & MARY IVY
HOUSE, SUNBURY ON THAMES. blt.
1692, on site of Historic CROMWELL
HOUSE: seat of the EARL OF ESSEX 1511–
1522. The grounds are not too awe-inspiring.
You can hang your washing out & swig
bottled beer under the great chestnut.
14 × 13ft. mini drawing rm., 2 bedrms., mod.
b. & k. Lse. 94 yrs. G.R. ONLY £15.

FLAT, Imposing 29ft drawing rm., dining rm. or 4th bedrm. 3 other gd. bedrms., 2 mod. bathrms. Steeped in culture – fellow tenants inc. famous playwright, an Air Marshal, 2 leading novelists & an OBE. The owner's wife is herself a prize winning Romantic Novelist ("You get high marks for chastity" said the judge.) A 10 yr. lse. for ONLY £2,850 – equal to ONLY £285 p.a.! Peppercorn rent.

FLAT BARGAIN, NW11. 3 mins. Brent Stn. Northern Line. Light grnd. flr. flat of vintage anti-nazi German foresaken the fatherland for the manufacture of 9 carat gold chastity belt padlocks, until, even more divided, their war-making potential is nobbled. Decent size sit. rm., small din. rm. dble bedrm., Kit. new Crane. A gift at £2,990.

ECCLESTON SQ. PENTHOUSE. Young English gentlewoman, fresh from Spanish Bull farm and vineyard, took this flat some months ago & unaccountably finds she prefers the climate on the Med., where she is returning. A spacious, lovely reception rm. with vast picture window (wld. make 2 rms.) leading to fine big sunbathing balcony, dble. bedrm. kit. bathrm. A glow of warmth is generated by the stairs, no lift. Use of Gdn. Sq. Lse. 80 yrs. G.R. ONLY £50. £4,700. TRY ANY OFFER.

CHEAP FLAT WITH POSH ADDRESS. A retrenching member of the Country Gentleman's Association, got as near the soil as he could when he took what is euphemistically termed *"The lower grnd. flr."* Still it is fairly light & very cosy & he has assiduously cultivated a crop of chives in a window box. Spacious dble. drawing rm., dble. bedrm., mod. bathrm., lab.-sav. kit. Well dec. in impeccable taste. Lse. 4½ yrs. ONLY £450 p.a.

BEER MAGNATE & refined lady sculptor & former teetotaler forced moved nearer his brewery sadly leave FASHIONABLE CHELSEA & 1st. flr. maisonnette. Own sunbathing roof-gdn with *"with real artificial grass"* 1st. flr. drawingrm., 2 bedrm., mod. bathr., new kit.-dining rm. will be made. Non-rep. lse. about 4½ yrs. ONLY £50 p.a. A GIFT AT £1,990.

> **THE TRAGEDY OF THE WORKING CLASSES IS THE POVERTY OF THEIR DESIRES** said KEIR HARDIE. I, too, have remarked their diffidence in bringing me their suburban houses of, say, £4,000 to £5,000 because they thought we dealt with *"posh"* people. This is not so. As a socialist I make only one distinction: that is between those who are honest – & those who are not: & with whom we prefer not to deal. ROY BROOKS.

"MAZURI SANA," muttered The White Settler from the Kenya Highlands when he saw & bought this shabby, spacious FAMILY HOUSE nr. FASHIONABLE BROCK GREEN & ST. PAUL'S SCHOOL. 5 admirable bedrms., drawing rm., dining rm., b'fast rm./kit. & scullery, bathrm. Garden. Pres. lse. to '75 G.R. ONLY £4 p.a. £3,350.

"THEATRICAL RATHER THAN CAMP" says Management Consultant who, since he moved in with working model has become overwhelmed by the population explosion & MUST SELL, THIS ELEGANT GROSVENOR CRES. MEWS. BELGRAVIA COTTAGE. Hidden, only abt. 50 yds. Hyde Park Corner, exclusive (only the best people are let in by the attendant at the gate). He says *"Neighbours are all film Stars, Models - or Chauffeurs."* Pleasant hall, charming dining rm., 3 bedrms., mod. bathrm., well fit. kit. Everything, including the occupants, is immaculate. Lse. 13½ yrs. ONLY £400 p.a. BARGAIN: £7,995.

FASHIONABLE BUT SLIGHTLY SORDID ISLINGTON. The somewhat decayed **PERIOD RES.** of genuine, but beardless painter (was multi-coloured, he says – probably having used it to wipe off the brushes – he had to remove it upon matrimony). 10 rms., water, gas & elec., but, of course, no bath. Period features include some artful graining of doors (due for a smart revival any time now). GARDEN backing onto an incredible forgotten ACRE of 18th-Century countryside, whose huge forest trees show the four seasons. ONLY £5,500 FHLD., try ANY, yes ANY offer.

FASHIONABLE CHELSEA. Untouched by the swinging world of fashion an early VIC lower middle class family dwelling, which has sunk to a working class tenement (2 lousy kits. & 3 sinks.) The decaying decor lit by *"High Speed Gas."* 6 main rms. & revolting appurtenances which could be turned into bathrm. & kit. I saw a bare footed school girl (or student teacher?) sweeping filth from rusty barbed wired playground through holes in the wall into the small back garden (sic) of this house. So the first thing to do is fill in the hole. A few doors away houses sell for over £18,000 & tarted up twin houses to this one make almost double the modest £8,500 asked for this dump. Lse. 51 yrs.

*"The most sought-after address in Islington
.... a title living next door and always a
Rolls or Bentley in the street. No, it is NOT
Balls Pond Road,"* said my client of his
GEORGIAN TOWN RESIDENCE upon
which he has squandered thousands of
pounds and his own exquisite taste. The
cocks in the guest shower room are plated
with gold. The owner's bathroom is so con-
trived that he can carry on watching the tely.
There is a magnificent entertaining room cum
grand dining room, over 30ft. (striking decor
a blend of mod. Swedish and Mid-West ranch
house) which merges into super lux. kitchen,
a Georgian drawing rm., the Master's double
bedroom, (cld. divide back into 2 bedrms,)
Immac new decor, full CENTRAL HEAT-
ING. Small garden dedicated to roses and
strawberries. Conservatory. FREEHOLD
£8,975.

**REVOLUTIONARY PIANO TEACHER
MUST SELL** convenient S.E.6. 1924
FAMILY HOUSE. 4 bedrms. Drawing rm.
takes grand piano. Gd. dining rm. 14 ft, kit.
Bathrm. Garden a 78ft. paradise for children
& free range guineapig, amidst a plethora
of crab (jelly) & cider apples, wine making
elderberries & weeds. GARAGE. RE-
DUCED TO £5,950 FOR QUICK SALE.

HYDE PK. Off. Lux. Sunny res. London's
most exclusive Mews, stiff with titles. Cobbled, overlking lovely grnds. of Royal Tox-
ophilite Society & Tennis Courts; ideal for
children – of all ages. Client tells me she
nightly hears 200 yr. old Tyburn Owl hooting
from her charming drawing rm., 2 bedrms.,
mod. bathrm., well fit. kit. Roof gdn. Gd.
decor. Lse. 17 yrs. ONLY £275 p.a. Going
Majorca. SACRIFICE £4,990.

RICH INVESTMENT. Lady of Title asks
us to flog Ebury St., BELGRAVIA, rooming
HOUSE. (1 treble, 1 single & 9 dble. rms., 3
bathrms.) *"All right,"* she says, *"as long as
you don't have to live there. All you have to do
is pop round once a week & collect the money
(over £118) in the season. Perfect housekeeper
& son do everything for £12 p.w."* £15,500 try
ANY offer. Contents £1,500. Long lse. to
2004. G.R. ONLY £120.

R∗B∗N B∗NH∗M C∗RT∗R the gigantic white trader – blanket and beads – and Rhodesian tobacco rancher returned to the old country to make his fortune *"Printing floral wraps for toilet paper"* and beautified this PIMLICO PERIOD TOWN HOUSE which, alas, his family have outgrown. Cent. Heat. elegant 30ft. first flr. drawing rm. to balcony, dining rm. study/5th bedrm., 4 bedrms., 3 new bathrms, bidet, lab. sav. kit. with b'fast bar, staff bed-sitting rm/games rm. Tiny paved yard. Lse. 78 yrs. £18,500.

HATCH END – THE PRIDE OF PINNER. Fashion model & Civil Engineer of those Cooling Towers that fell down (they forgot wind pressure, but no-one hurt – all at tea-break). MUST SELL FINE ARCHITECT BUILT, NEW ('63) SPACIOUS FAMILY HOUSE only 25 mins. Baker St. yet real nearby farm, where they get milk, seen from nursery. Georgian in style, it impresses all the neighbours. SUPERB 31ft. Drawing rm. to terrace & 70ft. garden, trees, fruit & flowers. 4 Dble. bedrms., 2 lux. bathrms., super fit. kit. FHLD £9,995.

KNIGHTSBRIDGE FLAT of KL∗M∗NI∗SKI the fashionable photographer of guided missiles, racing cars and specially selected perfectly proportioned but tiny girl models to scale for modern, mass produced sports jobs. SUNNY, QUIET 3rd. flr. (no lift). Charming drawing rm., dining rm. or 3rd. bedrm. 2 other dble. bedrms. Large, mod. bath/dressing rm. avec bidet. Big kit. SACRIFICE £2,995.

HISTORIC MONUMENT: Granddaughter of Painter in Ordinary to H.M. QUEEN VICTORIA (*"The Soul's Awakening – at least you could see what it was ..."*) & an interesting Prima-Donna offers her XVIIth Cent. cottage res. Enchanting with its bow window & rounded gable. Poshest part FASHIONABLE MARLOW, quiet cul-de-sac with slipway. Dining rm. or study, country sized b'fast rm. kit. Charming 1st flr. drawing rm. 3 bedrms., fairly mod. bathrm. Don't expect not to have to spend something & the garden is a jungle but the price of £5,525 FREEHOLD is ridiculously low for the fabric of history & may be a bit of rot.

CRI DE COEUR FROM NEWPORT, MON. Redhead sculptress, trumpeter, jazz pianist & Psychologist seek Victorian house, pref. big attic, in refined neighbourhood. London area. Abt. £7,000. ROY BROOKS.

£3,995 FREEHOLD. ANTIQUARIAN PROUDLY OFFERS his ghastly Peckham house. Almost innocent of plumbing, no bathrm. – bodily ablutions confined to a couple of sinks & the canal at the bottom of the garden. 8 fair sized rooms. As the artists have already moved into Peckham it is only a matter of time before they are followed by the fringe professions, Stage, Tely and Advertising – with the Chelsea type of monied intellectual snob breathing on their necks – then a dump like this will be worth well over £10,000. MOVE QUICKLY.

FASHIONABLY GRIMY CHELSEA. Elegant 1st. flr. balcony FLAT: GUNTER GROVE (soon to be one way & much quieter – everything going to the right: like the Labour Party's DISCIPLINARY GROUP: pledged to expunge Socialism). Drawing rm., Adam mantel, 2 gd. bedrms., mod. b. & k. Lse. 95 yrs. G.R. £10. £4,550. Try any offer as International Handler must move quick.

WESTMORELAND TERRACE, WESTMINSTER, S.W.1. MOD. LUXURY ARCHITECT RES., one of four built where three stood before, so don't expect big rms; but ideal for, say, Japanese family. Owner, from N. Australia has no objection to Japs – in Pimlico. Elegant 1st. flr. "L" drawing rm., dining rm., 3 bedrms., mod. bathrm., well-fit. b'fast rm., kit., clkrm. VIEW OF RIVER from 2 rms. – just. GARAGE. A GIFT AT £10,550 FHLD.; TRY ANY OFFER.

£3,995. BLOSSOM-LINED PALACE GARDEN TERRACE, KENSINGTON. Campden Hill, resort of the rich. The gracious & comfortable family house of Socialist Lady Journalist & Copywriter who worked on the glowing ads. for those first cornets. (Most Ad. men sensibly don't patronise their own wares). Exterior completely redecorated: inside good. Beautiful Drawing rm., french windows over garden – French beans, elderly Hydrangea & Nasturtium. Gd. dining rm. to concealed lift to fine big B'fast rm./kit. bay window. 5 g. bedrms., 3 bathrms. Church Commissioner Lse. to 1974 (with God on your side you should get extension). ONLY £212 p.a.

FASHIONABLE CHELSEA. Fine 8 rm. house. 2 bathrms. Consent to let rms. (Estimated income £1,500 p.a. plus owner's suite; 3 gd. rms.) £3,000 spent bringing up to her own high standards by friend of Royalty. (Trekked 800 miles on horseback with 100 bearers & baby brother in meat safe to make African camp for Edward, Prince of Wales, & took *"elevenses"* – stewed duck served in chamberpot, with Great Queen Magui, aged 102: 13 husbands – 2 thrown by herself to the crocodiles, & who had tin of sardines & Golden Syrup on the table to show how English she was ...) Lse. 10 yrs. Thought renewable. G.R. only £20 p.a. £7,995, try ANY offer.

CHISWICK. Leading Architect, who did the publicity of London Ctte. for Nuclear Disarmament (I hope this cranky aversion to genocide won't blight his career), taking up important provincial appointment, must sell GRAND WHITE PAINTED EDWARDIAN FAMILY HOUSE with its splendid 1st floor drawing rm., pale grey & pine panelling; gd. dining rm. extra recep. rm. as playroom, direct to garden, apple & pear trees. B'fast rm. Kit. 3 gd. bedrms., bathrm. *"Rather decrepit – or charmingly old fashioned; whichever way you look at it ..."* FREEHOLD £6,950.

H.R.H. PRINCESS X is graciously pleased to flog her beautiful luxury FLAT in splendid PALACE GATE KENSINGTON, MOD BLOCK. & accept a very mod. fig. for f. & f. It is possible to make a very suitable regal entry down the spiral stair to the noble dble. reception rm. overlkg. Gdns. 2 bedchambers, mod. tiled bathrm., kit., stainless steel sink &c. Excellent cpds. throughout. GARAGE &/OR FALLOUT SHELTER BELOW. ONLY £650 p.a.

**POISED BETWEEN THE REGENCY ELE-
GANCE** of King George The Good & the Victorian horror of Camden Town. (Few hundred yds.
Regent's Pk.). Another 7 rm., b. & k. res. being
reconstructed by a worthy Estate whose standards
are high & whose prices are low. Own Gdn. Lse. 80
yrs. Say £4,500 if the owner likes the look of you.

"Be it never so humble . . .": The Stockbroker's
dream of home: **CHELSEA.** Brand-new res. yet
with drawing-rm. vast enough for expense account entertaining. 3 bedrms. with large fit. wardrobe cupbds., b. & k. No expense spared. Even
the lav, done in historic handblocked Tartan
paper. A chic black & white as original, blocked
for Queen Victoria in Royal Stuart, deemed unsuit-
able. Give us time & your Clan & you can have a
bespoke job. Only £5,350. 40 yrs. G.R. abt. £26.
Unaffected by the Credit Squeeze. Brooks can, of
course, get you an enormous Mortgage.

SELF-RAISING MILLER COMPELLED TO
MOVE TO LARGER HOUSE, DUE TO
ALARMING GROWTH OF FAMILY which
therefore sacrifices what every Stockbroker & his
undomesticated wife desires; an easily run non-
basement MODERN CHELSEA HOUSE. 4
bedrms., 4 telephones, study or 5th bedrm., an elegant drawing rm. & a comfortable dining rm., 2
rather good mod tiled bathrms., & kit., tiled with
stainless steel sink, etc. POLISHED OAK FLRS.
CENTRAL HEATING, WONDERFUL CUP-
BOARDS. GARDEN. Lse. to 1997 G.R. £16, yet
ONLY £8,750.

BRILLIANT BEARDED ARCHITECT BE-
LIEVING MIDDLE CLASS deserves something
better than its usual habitat, designs 4 Impeccable
HOUSES: ONLY £3,775 FREEHOLD. (Some
have even been snapped up by Gentlepeople realiz-
ing same in Knightsbridge costs £12,000 ONLY
ONE LEFT!) 3 Good bed. 2 rec. opening as one
great rm. super k. & b. LARGE GARAGE. Good
Gardens. Guaranteed NO leaded windows, tiled
or brick chimneypieces – & no door chimes . . .
View Healthy high Sunny Site Sun. or Monday.
Westwood Park, near Horniman Park, S.E.23, nr.
glorious country around Dulwich College. A
matter of mins. by Train to Town.

MEMBER OF SECRET SOCIETY MUST SELL MOD. (built between two German wars) RES. Popular NORBURY. "Everyone in Victoria train gets off here …" 15 mins. 3 Bed. 2 rec. tiled b. & k. CHW. Gd. order; money lavished on improvements. Plain Glass replaced by leaded lights. Gdn. GARAGE. Incomparable value at £2,150.

IF YOU WISH TO LIVE DECENTLY behind the modest and unobjectionable façade of an early Victorian house in which the remnants of Georgian good taste linger; have a family or aspire to lodgers of the gentler sort, and not much cash, you could do worse than look at OVAL RD., Regent's Park, Ter., N.W.1. Conscientiously modernised and reconstructed where necessary, using the finest materials, including papers originally commissioned by HM King George IV. 6, or are there about 7? rms, some of them, in a way, rather fine, mod. b. & k. Tiny gdn. Only £5,250 for 80 yrs. A low G.R. Simply ENORMOUS Mortgage. There may be a caretaker here on Sunday, on the other hand there may not.

ERSTWHILE MAKER OF SECRET WEAPONS TAKING UP DRINK forced sacrifice far below cost, for immediate sale, so he can capture the Xmas trade. For those who yen for the romantic, if smelly, past is not gratified by Stockbroker's Tudor. THE REAL THING (circa Henry VIII). Small Farm House in glorious acre skirting ever-open meadows 45 mins. your clerkly stool. Exquisitely restored by local *Craftsmen*, over £2,500 spent! 3 Bedrms., dressing-rm., lux. tiled bathrm., 2 lovely rec., super kitchen, dble. sink unit. Piping hot water & everywhere suffused in warm glow. Enchanting original small galleried staircase. Only the Telyantennae prods into the nasty present. £3,975 FHLD. TRY ANY OFFER.

READY FOR FILM STAR &/OR SUCCESSFUL STOCKBROKER TO WALK INTO. The finishing touches are being laid on this NEW CHELSEA LUXURY HOUSE by a Master Architect who has all too skilfully blended The Contemporary with The Classical to harmonise with its surroundings: 3 Bedrooms, vast Reception, Gleaming Parquet, Kitchen and Bathroom, £5,350.

STOP PRESS. LITTLE OPERA SINGER going into the jungle, and as she will not be returning from Hollywood for some time, she is having to sacrifice ONE OF THE BEST HOUSES IN KENSINGTON with certainly THE BEST GARDEN, which, although very large, with lovely lawns, plethora flowers and colony of chows, is easy to maintain. 5 perfect bed 2 glorious rec. opening into one splendid 40 ft. room. The enchanting music room, 2 good bathrooms. Gnd flr. kit. PLUS lower grd. flr. Flat for sub-letting extra children or staff; but daily can cope. £6,950 leasehold. TRY ANY, ANY OFFER. If you like the house and are socially and financially acceptable to the ground landlord, and will maintain legacy of daily carrot to milkman's horse, we will go into full details of lease.

£1,700 leasehold. S.W.11. Just over river from Chelsea. Neighbouring, and not inferior to, house for which frozen applicant camped all night outside office. Modernised with rather more regard to luxury than taste. 3 beds, 2 rec., mod. B. & K. Stainless steel sink unit. PLUS income from entirely separate S/C flat. Big Mortgage.

WE ALWAYS THOUGHT "nobody lives South of the River," but the fierce competition to buy last week's Clapham Common bargain encourages us to offer another to those of our readers bizarre enough (or just hard up) to rub shoulders with the lower middle classes. A NON-BASE HOUSE on 2 flrs., as 2 FLATS, which could be s/c. 1st flr. VACANT: reconstructed and redec. Attractive lounge, as they call the drawing rm. out here, good dining rm., DOUBLE bedrm., new mod, bathrm., small lab-sav. kit. Stainless steel sink unit. PLUS small income from grnd. flr. flat which owner says is likely to be vacant in near future. (Is this the new Rent Bill casting its sinister shadow ahead – or have the steps been soaped?) HOUSE in excellent state of repair, new wiring, plumbing and overhauled roof.

BENEVOLENT LANDLORD (a rara avis indeed) employs his great wealth in splendidly reconstructing and modernising PERIOD RES. in the seedy purlieu of Pimlico, which has been coming up since House of Hanover occupied those 17 acres off Grosvenor Place. It is becoming increasingly respectable among the less affluent M.P.s who can walk to work. Even Labour Members are moving into the nicer parts. 2/3 reception rms., 4/5 bedrms., new mod. b. & k. Lse. 80 yrs at only £35 p.a. G.R. Price £5,250. Large mortgage available.

FASHION DESIGNER & VAN DRIVER offers her amusing little MEWS COTTAGE, decor somewhat party-worn, but some interesting graffiti. Drawing rm & dining rm., both wood-block flrs. 2 bedrms., mod. bathrm., & kit. HOLLAND PARK. Sacrifice £1,450. Rent & Rates only £210 p.a. Lse. to 1967, when Labour should be in a position to look after tenant's interests, providing you haven't been "cleaned up" by one of the new H-bombs.

CHELSEA. Still probably the most popular residential area, despite the infiltration of middle-class elements. A couple of nice little NEW HOUSES. The exteriors have a refined nouveau Georgian façade, which should appeal to those of uncertain taste who prefer to play safe. A really spacious & potentially delightful drawing rm., 2 decent bedrms, (the best is enormous) & a 3rd ("If you please, ma'am, it was a very little one"), mod. bathrm., lab-sav. kit. Good-sized gardens, the best is enormous for Town, full of possibilities – and the mess left by the builders. A gift at £5,250. 40 yrs. Low G.R. Keys Office. Peer at outsides if you wish, they're at bottom Gertrude St.

£1,995 FHLD. NEVER ANY PLANNING TROUBLE ABOUT THIS HOUSE. It's exactly like its neighbours, & nobody could ever accuse it of being original, interesting or even attractive. All too solidly built in '05. Aircraft Executive & artist son have done best with tasteful interior. Mod. bathrm. 2 good rec. rooms, 3 nice bedrms., B'fast rm. Kit Recently redec. & re-plumbed. The gdn looks horrible, but so would you if you'd been neglected for 20 yrs. A fantastic bargain for the lower economic classes who don't take this sort of paper, but perhaps in the course of a fish supper . . .

£3,300 FHLD. BARONET'S BARGAIN. *Me*: "I see the hall is described as Panelled; what sort?" *Sir Richard*: "The cheapest possible, I should think." Me: "Are the 2 bedrms double?" Sir R.: "Just about." Me: "And the Drawing rm?" Sir R.: "Three people in it & you'd feel crowded." There is a small sun rm, b'fast rm kit, & what Sir Richard proudly claims to be the only bathrm in the street, but I think he's exaggerating; his aunt has stuffed the gdn with corms. £500 recently spent on fabric. Nr gd day sch. (St. Pauls).

ONE OF THE OLDEST & MOST LUCRATIVE PROFESSIONS IN THE WORLD. A CHELSEA ANTIQUE BUSINESS specialising in the sale of dwarf Frenchy tables for the Knightsbridge élite to perch their tely on. SHOP & 2 small rear rms. SILLY SACRIFICE £1,475. Lse 11 yrs. Rent only £250 p.a.

LADY OF TITLE, a retired Suffragist & active Family Planning expert, is moving to flat & must sacrifice one of the loveliest of modernised PERIOD HOUSES in CHELSEA'S BEST GDN SQ. (As residents, not absentee grnd Landlords, own it: it is superb). Entrance Drawing rm, fine dining rm, her Ladyship's boudoir & tely rm ("It's educating the upper classes even if they're too snobbish to admit it," she avers) 4 perfect bedrms, 2 mod bathrms, mod lab-saving kit, super stainless steel sink unit, ckr. & frig. V. gd decor. Small gdn. A GIFT AT £10,500 FHLD.

IDEAL FOR A RICH STOMACH WITH A TASTE FOR BUSINESS. A GORGEOUS LITTLE RESTAURANT (& s/c furn mais over, lets 12/15 gns p.w.). Delicate Noble-woman unable cope rush of business must sacrifice. Super kit. 4 sinks, 2 big ckrs, still-rm, exciting decor; seats 30, easily & cheaply fixed to take 80. Lavish equip. Gaggia coffee mach. Posh patrons. HYDE PK, nr Marble Arch. £7,950 lock, stock & barrel, or owner wld strip if wanted for any other purpose.

H.R.H. PRINCE C. instructs us to sell modern TOWN RES, KINGSINGTON. The Princess, an English girl who happened to be teaching English in Siam & H.R.H. (*now civilised & holding down a steady job in an Ad. Agency*) fell in love with the decor – dirty great cabbage roses all the way up the stairs. 27ft. dble drawing rm, PARQUET. 5 bedrms. vivid pink tiled bathrm. Kit. pt. CENT. HEAT. GARAGE Long lse 62 yrs. G.R. ONLY £28 p.a. SACRIFICE £13,995 (Re-decorated by, say, a rich vulgar business man should realise Twenty thousand pounds).

MR. PH*I*P H*RB*N has asked us to sell his magnificent new house in W.1. I have never seen this gentleman (my children say "If daddy dies, & mummy marries again – may we have television?"), but I am told he cooks &, from an ad I saw, it appears he does it all with a pinch of salt. This is borne out by the truly superb kit dble sink, mixer valve, Wastemaster, Dishmaster, 3 speed extractor fans, 3 cookers, special curry corner. Wine cellar, 3,000 bottles + or − 5 deg F., No vibration. There are also 3 bedrms (dble column thermometer showing inside and outside temps) 2 superlux bathrms. A gorgeous Drawing rm & study. TV. ITV. VHF aerial intakes. Bookshelves. Large dining Room. Rose clad. floodlit terrace gdn. Fountain & concealed "drinks" frig. The parquet gleams & the heating is central. Foundations alone cost £2,000. Garage. All this gracious living, for less than cost, a mere £19,995. Lse 77 yrs. £200 p.a.

"WHERE HAVE ALL THE GENTRY GONE – THEY'VE GONE TO TOOTING EVERYONE . . ." "A butler opened the door" says the ebulient young mother of five when she bought this GRAND VICTORIAN DETACHED TOOTING BEC FAMILY HOUSE. Now, with GAS CENT HEAT, etc., she runs it with only a daily. With the spacious grandeur of an age past, it has 7 bedrms, 3 bathrms with one super new one, 1st flr drawing rm commanding an L.C.C. park like vista across the Bec Common, substantial dining rm, study leading to conservatory, B'fast rm & kit. Sequestred GARDEN. DBLE GARAGE. Only 10 mins train Victoria. SACRIFICE £10,975 FHLD.

**FASHIONABLE REGENTS PARK SIDE OF
PRIMROSE HILL.** Gorgeous 1st flr FLAT
with large, lovely drawing-rm. Vast windows vir-
tually flr to ceiling. *"Wonderful view of sunsets
thro, the tracery of the trees & model girls being
photographed on the hill ... the distant mating cry
of the Hyena in the still of a summer night ..."*
says Cultured Delian & Top Ad Copy-writer –
Elec Shaver, pens & Airlines *"Crashes? Better to
kill them than just frighten them – don't talk ..."*
Super dble bedrm with disrobing annexe with
large fitted wdrbe en route for very comfortable
modn bathrm. Super kitn. Wrighton fittings,
waste disposal unit, extrator fan. Decor excellent.
Lse 96 yrs. G.R. £75 p.a. PRICE £5,995.

GRACIOUS LIVING IN W.14. (opp. Olympia) M*CH*L *H*LR*YD'S sunny spacious top (2nd & 3rd flr) Mais *"A very scholarly looking flat"* says the Lady Medievalist who cooks *"The 20ft Draw rm study where 'Lytton Strachey' was written, piles of dreadful books & papers littered everywhere, shared with 10 (at last count) guinea-pigs."* 2 Bedrms, wall length ftmt. Bathrm *"Simply terrible."* B'fast rm Kit. 67 yrs. GR ONLY £40. BARGAIN at £5,995.

DR. X GOING ABROAD TO CARRY ON CANCER RESEARCH (after speaking to him no one in his or her right mind would ever smoke another cigarette) MUST SELL superbly blt. mod.-looking 1924 MUSWELL HILL family hse. Fine open prospect o'er Cricket Grnds. (bowls for the more energetic) to HIGHGATE. Modernised & well cared for. Ent. hall, oak flr. Spacious drawing rm. to gdn. Pleasant dining rm. 4 bedrms., 1 with super balcony to watch cricket. $\frac{1}{2}$ tiled bathrm. Big well fit. b'fast. rm./kit. OIL FIRED CENT. HEAT. Interesting 130ft gdn., lawn, fruit trees. GARAGE. Lse. 980 yrs. G.R. ONLY £12. BARGAIN £8,995.

EXOTIC LUXURY IN MILL HILL, few mins. beautiful Green Belt Country, fast trains Town. Gleaming white SANTA BARBARA Spanish style house approached by sweeping drive. Lawns, aviary, a rich profusion of fruit & flowers, greenhse. Gorgeous big secluded gdn. *"Every morning I sunbathe in the nude on the terrace & bathe in the lily pool which could be used for swimming,"* says owner, a lady of Spanish blood. Clkrm., charming 20ft. drawing rm. to sun loggia, b'fastrm, beamed dining rm. or study, 4 main bedrms., dressing rm., or 5th bedrm., lux. bathrm., shower, lab.-sav. kit., stainless steel sink unit. etc., etc. CENT HEAT. Excellent decor. 2 GARAGES, TERRIFIC BARGAIN £15,995 FREEHOLD and try ANY offer as client is waiting to fly off to Majorca.

I DESPISE DISHONEST DESCRIPTION. (My first Tely Commercial "Oil is O.K. for Central Heating if you don't mind the pong of diesel fuel" was my last). Hope you don't find anything worse than spelling mistakes in our FREE list of 309 hses. & 141 flats. Many of the best haven't been hawked around as we've sole agency – but don't necessarily need one to sell yours.

HOUSEBOAT, SUPER PRIV. MOORING, RICHMOND ON THAMES. Little ex-WREN fell in love with this sleek spacious 70ft. Motor Torpedo Boat. *"I think it was built end of war so hasn't killed anyone ..."* Sons now gone ashore and MUST SELL. 50 knots claimed before Rolls engine removed. Claimed one of best conversions. Ent. hall, SUN LOUNGE, fine dining salon, cocktail bar, well fit. galley, stainless steel sink, 3 gd. cabin bedrms, gd. bathrm., heated towel rail. SACRIFICE £2,850 and TRY ANY OFFER, inc. all the super fit. furn. Suitable refined pop singer, Film or telly Star – or anyone likes to be thought one (convenient TWICKENHAM STUDIOS).

"EVEN SOPHISTICATED GIRL MODELS ARE IMPRESSED when they see my 28 x 16½ft. Studio-cum-Drawing rm. with slick super-mod. kit., dble. stainless steel sinks, etc." says artistic Northumberland Fashion photographer. Close Oval & West End (walking distace Parliament), this LAMBETH PERIOD RES. has 4 bedrms., LARGE shower room with Vanitory unit & bidet. PLUS GD. INCOME £7 p.w. from ideal S/c base. FLAT tenants. (VAC. POSS. IF REQ.). Drawing rm., 2 bedrms., mod. bathrm., kit. Gd. 70ft. walled gdn. BARGAIN £9,825 FREEHOLD.

WEALTHY YOUNG DILET-TANTE, delighted with speed with which we disposed of his Mayfair mais., informs us that everything including the gas stove was taken over, save for his magnificent collection of antique Chinese Jade, Ivory and Rose quartz, which he must flog as he is now interested in something else. Worth nearly £2,000. Sacrifice, £1,100; or wld. separate. Par example: a grovelling courtier, price £35. (300 old Ming Ivory. Nothing new in the world – is there?)

£2,990 ! ONE OF THE POSHEST PARTS OF LONDON. Rembrandt Close, Holbein Pl., S.W.1. In the rich environs of Sloane St. New ('62) Town House. 24ft. split level drawing rm., well fit. kit., 4 bedrms., fit. wdrbs., 2 mod. bathrms. Elec. CENT. HEAT. GARAGE, Our client Captain X, a rich, well connected youngish Conservative says quite frankly the house isn't good enough for him & as money doesn't really interest him he'll take a nominal £2,990 from the first decent chap whose face fits. Lse. 13½ yrs. ONLY £600 p.a.

£5,995 FHLD.! FASHIONABLE DUL-WICH. Fin de siècle family house of Scots Banker. Less taciturn, his Asiatic Russian Lady describes how she reached this sequestered spot (miles of country-like walks, 12 mins., Lon. Br.) from a revolutionary infancy in the Urals, via Siberia in a cattle train. Written up, she says, in GOOD HOUSEKEEPING. *"Photos of children hanging from apple trees in the big garden."* Ent. hall, PARQUET. drawing rm., formal dining rm. used as son's 5th bedrm., b'fast rm. leading to kit., 4 other bedrms., bathrm. Wide Garage & the 2 prize-winning Mini-Coopers sprawl across the drive.

FASH. FULHAM.   Interesting 19th-cent. House
with Royal associations; the res. of THOS. BICK-
LEY, Head Plasterer to H.M. QUEEN VIC-
TORIA: The Royal Coat of Arms proudly em-
blazoned outside (it was also home of Lily
Langtry the Jersey Lily). Base.: big front rm. &
tiny rm., bathrm., w.c., big kit Grnd.: 2 gd. inter
comm. rms. with dble drs. for Formal Entertaining. 24ft.? 2 fine marble chmnypces, small kit.,
w.c., $\frac{1}{2}$ land.: 25ft. secret rm. for informal entertaining (client discovered hidden trap dr. in bathrm.
when she was 4). 1st flr.: 2 lge. rms., period
chmnypces., big kit., period bathrm. and w.c. 2nd
flr.: 3 big rmns., 1 for sun lover with wall of glass
to sunbathing balcony, also sun roof with views,
gd. sized gdn. of flowers, lawn, imposing statue of
Mercury on column, space for car. Small outbuild-
ing in Gothick style – the old plaster rm.

DR X & GIRL who does *"those foreign Art Books"* forced relinquish FINE ENT FLR FLAT in heart of FASHIONABLE BLACKHEATH. (Handsome mid-19th Cent hse close The Paragon) Fine 21 × 15½ft Reception rm, 2 gd dble Bedrooms, large mod Bathrm, Kit. Full use magnificent 200ft garden. Lse 84 yrs. GR £25 p.a. £5,575.

FILTHY OLD HOUSE – FASHIONABLE CHELSEA – Preserved as of Architectural Interest – God Know's Why. Providing you have enough patience and cash wld make: 3 bedrms. 27ft L-drawing rm. a dining room, 1 or 2 bathrms., kit. The horrible patch of weed, refuse infected earth behind wld make a lovely – Gdn – maybe. Lease, 51 years. G.R. ONLY £80. A gift at £8,550.

CAN MIDDLE CLASS MAN ASPIRE TO ANYTHING HIGHER THAN THIS? (When owner saw draft he demurred at *Middle Class. "There are,"* he says, *"Real Lords on the Estate."*) A New ('63) RANCH STYLE DET. HOUSE in *private* drive *"Wiv wooded environs."* In FASHIONABLE DULWICH only 12 mins. Victoria. Clkrm. Fine LARGE split level drawing rm. & dining rm., study, or extra bedrm., 4 gd. bedrms., fit. wdrbs., BIG boxrm., 2 LUX bathrms., shower, super Wrighton fit. b'fast rm./kit. GLEAM. PARQUET. CENT. HEAT. Fully stocked gdn. ABUTTING WOOD. DBLE GARAGE (takes his Vintage Rolls & another) ONLY £17,850.

FINE PERIOD TOWN HOUSE off Brompton Rd., KNIGHTSBRIDGE. Superbly modernised recently by rich restless couple, the gifted RADA actress who does the tely bird seed ads – beautifully, & Top Ad. man (*"Batteries & beer"*) who says *"From our bedrm we can see the minarets of Harrods touched with sunlight . . ."* Thousands & thousands, & thousands spent achieving perfection. NEW CENTRAL HEATING. The elegant 27ft 1st flr. Drawing rm, PARQUET. Gd. Dining rm. Restful Study. 5 gd. Bedrms, ample fit cpbds. 2 MOD Bathrms. Super-lab-sav B'fast rm kit. Decor, of course, impeccable. Small gdn, with a rather weedy fig tree which, in its ambition to reach the top at all costs, has failed to reproduce itself properly. LONG lse. 56 yrs. G.R. ONLY £50. A BARGAIN AT £21,875 but TRY ANY offer. MUST BE SOLD, ALBEIT AT A LOSS.

£3,250! Even try offer, FASHIONABLE DULWICH. Owner writes: *"Decayed Dentist Deserting Dulwich Village for Devon."* Mr Lowman inspected the comfortable late Vict. family home since '27 of this former member of Common Wealth, a humane Socialist who says *"I don't even like to see the News on Television – the World is in such a muddle . . ."* Spacious pleasant drawing rm., to gdn., large dining rm., b'fast rm. & kit., 4 gd. bedrms., bathrm. Garden now neglected. GARAGE – new £100 roof – & space 2nd GARAGE. 50% short mortge. poss. avail. Lse. 21 yrs. G.R. ONLY £8.

HYDE PARK PLACE. 1st flr FLAT FULL GORGEOUS VIEWS Sth o'er HYDE PARK quiet & sunny behind dble-glazing in front, & behind, acres of quiet open country – 100 yards Marble Arch. Noble trees, a Collie romping thro' the fading flowers & runner beans, one notices, amid the brambles the odd tombstone (Most are stacked or cemented in – to buttress the basement area) the well cut ancient lettering defying the indifference of time. Part given to pleasure, 2 hard tennis courts. Decent sized Ent hall, Drawing rm roughtly 25 × 21ft. PARQUET, door to miniscule balcony. 2 dble bedrms, BIG fit wdrbs, mod tiled Bathrm & well equipped Kit. Lse 33 yrs. G.R. £100 p.a. £5,995.

FASHIONABLE ISLINGTON. Modernised period residence. A former MIKVA, i.e., JEWISH BATH HOUSE (The friendly jibe *"always washing themselves"* stems from their ancient practice of *washing*, foreign to many of their neighbours). CENTRAL HEATING. Drawing rm., with dble doors to dining rm., study, FINE BIG bkfst. rm./kit., 7 bedrooms, 2 bathrooms. Small garden with hedge. Decor. mixed. Lse. 68 yrs. G.R. only £25. BARGAIN £9,995.

MR KENNETH TYNAN'S FLAT. To use a four-letter word the address is POSH. *"Ideal,"* he says *'For an autograph collector – opposite the Connaught Hotel."* Spacious, 2nd flr. mansion block, MOUNT ST., MAYFAIR. Elegant 25ft. drawing rm., flr-to-ceiling bow window, imposing formal dining rm., study, 3 bedrms., plus dressing rm., mod. bathrm., b'fast rm./kit., twin stainless steel sink, boxrm. Lse. 5ys. ONLY £875 p.a.

A SCHOOL FRIEND OF MY SISTER WANTED TO MARRY AN ENGINEER. Her shocked mum said *"What will ESHER say?"* Its now more plebeian, but still nr real country. Almost opp CLAREMONT LAKE. Secluded ½ ACRE gdn (Georgian loose box), lrge gravelled drive. Emigrating adman's modernised early 19th cent period res. OIL CENT HEAT. Canopied Ent. Big rec hall/study. Elegant drawing rm. Dining rm to gdn. Big study/plyrm. 4 gd bdrms (3 DBLE). 2 mod bathrms BIDET. B'fast rm/kit. 33ft dble GARAGE. Lawns, flowers, fruit cage, asparagus bed, peaches. SACRIFICE £15,950 FHLD.

ONE OF THE FILTHIEST HOUSES I'VE SEEN FOR A LONG TIME. A crumbling corner PERIOD RES. There are many things that can be said about FASHIONABLE PIMLICO: Dingy, for instance. 9 rms (Some quite fine altho' they've kept coal in a bedrm & the Drawing rm chimney piece is sprawled across the flr.) Built in an age of elegance, contemporary I should think, with Emperor LOUIS PHILLIPE, to restore it is about the only challenge left to a rich young couple today. ONLY £8,450. Lse 80 yrs. G.R. ONLY £70.

£2,250! SACRIFICE FAR BELOW COST. KENSINGTON. SLOPES FASHIONABLE CAMPDEN HILL. TOWN PERIOD RES run as Physiotherapy Clinic by Scots Clansman & lady Alsatian, the Countess G. Von K. Starting at the bottom, they offer: Dungeon like cellar with massive chain fixed to wall. A large room which opens into paved garden. Large pt tiled kit-b'fst rm. Old Bathrm. Ent Flr: Clkrm, 2 Rec rms with glazed drs form MAGNIFICENT RM, prob over 40ft. A small rm with fit basin, 1st Flr: 20ft Drawing rm, 2 Bedrms, basins, Bathrm. 2nd Flr: 3 rms as yet undec. A LOT OF THE BEST IS NEWLY DEC. Lse 8 years (As it's Church Comms, one hopes to God that they'll extend). ONLY £880 p.a.

FASHIONABLE BATTERSEA. Little backwater foot of PIG HILL, fenced in with pickle barrel staves, the quaint COTTAGE STUDIO & gallery of remarkable Liverpudlian nude-landscape painter (not nudes on landscape but nudes turned *into* landscapes) – the accent has gone but the hair cut still remains. Front studio or sit rm. 2 bedrms. dining rm. or 3rd bedrm. New midget bathrm & kit. Pretty well re-blt, all grubby white decor & natural wood. SPACE DBLE GARAGE. Prize winning novel of 1964 was written in top back rm by nobleman's heiress seeking local colour. A GIFT AT £3,995 FHLD.

BARGAIN. ENORMOUSLY SPACIOUS super, but somewhat scruffy 1st Flr FLAT FASHIONABLE FROGNAL, HAMPSTEAD, N.W.3. Never looked back since RAMSEY MAC (*"All the Duchess's will want to **** me"*) lived in rd. MUST BE SOLD by *"Most socially engaged of Science Fiction writers"* (vide VOGUE) J*HN BR*NN*R who says *"Rather done it a generation from now when they have sorted out some of the more pressing problems."* (Like food, shelter, health & hope for the hopeless millions? Personally what I'm doing this weekend is more important to me than the moonshot, but hope poor Collins & Co fare better than the monkey. REB) 4 rms (3 HUGE). Bathrm & SHOWER, SPACIOUS kit. dble stainless sink. 200ft unkempt Gdn, residents have their own private parts. Lse 95 yrs. GR £550. ONLY £7,995.

A 1483 MANOR HOUSE IN N.W.2. Former res. of QUEEN ELIZABETH'S ½ BROTHER, CROMWELL'S General, SIR WM. ROBERTS & BARTHOLOMEW WILLESDEN who *gave* his name to this delectable suburb – even the factory opposite gave birth to the 1st Bentley. A superbly preserved beamed detached large family hse., used as Guest House, or ideal posh Restaurant & owner's res. Clkrm., gorgeous 22ft open plan drawing rm., quaint spiral 2nd stair to bedrms., large dining rm., impressive log f'place, doors to Garden – ENORMOUS apple tree (only abt. ¼ acre left of 500 acres). The library, 6 bedrms. (5 dble.), 2 perfectly gd. attic bedrms., bathrm., super country-house flagged kit.-b'fast. rm. stainless steel sink, £200 p.a. from quite sep. small business prem. attached. Lse to Sept. '68. FANTASTIC BARGAIN £9,995 FHLD.

HUNGARIAN RETURNING TO IBIZA WITH
GENTLEWOMAN FORCES QUICK SALE OF
TYPICAL UPPER CLASS 2nd flr FLAT IN
PHILLIMORE GDNS, KENSINGTON. In
rather imposing period house. Very pleasant
sunny Drawing rm. 2 DOUBLE Bedrms, fit
cpbds. Mod Bathrm & kit. Everything beautifully
maintained. Perfect daily would stay for approved
purchaser. Lse 31 yrs. GR & Maint £176 p.a.
£8,750 try ANY offer.

DESPERATE ENGLISHMAN & FRENCH GIRL WOULD CONSIDER ANYTHING SORDID – they missed house we sold in Lilyville Rd. 3 months ago. FULHAM or similar. It really *is* urgent, please respond.

ATTRACTED BY THE COVER, read "THE NAKED APE" & am pleased to offer residence of decadent descendant. (Apes seek only to frighten their enemies – not kill. U.S., U.S.S.R., El Fatah et all please copy.) D*SM*ND M*RR*S going Oxford. FORCED SELL 100-yr.-old DET. FAMILY HOUSE (BARNET) reconstructed regardless of cost, retaining Period features. An immaculate conception, high, healthy, gorgeous views across to Hadley Woods & Barnet Church. BIG secluded, exciting 130ft. walled gdn., 3 levels, HIGH HEDGES (to stop the deer escaping). Wide ent. hall, ELEGANT LOFTY drawing rm. to balcony, thence gdn., BIG library, for those who never get beyond the Sunday reviews it wld. make a fine tely rm. or extra dble. bedrm., small study. 4 bedrms. (3 DBLE.), master bedrm. has dress. rm., wdrbs., BIDET, LUX. BATHRM., vanitory unit, shower, black suite & tiled, b'fast. rm., kit., BIG cellar rm., super playrm? (no windows). FULL GAS-FIRED CENT. HEAT. GARAGE. Potentially a historic house for ONLY £15,995 FHLD.

ERSTWHILE CONDUCTOR ROYAL PHILHARMONIC (MADE GOOD COMPOSING TOP TELYAD MUSIC Motor oil to cholesterol-rich edible fats) offers rich Vic. fmly. res. EALING almost opposite NIAGARA HOUSE which BLONDIN bought from proceeds, nr. Studios & 10 mins. train TV. Centre. Wide ent. hall. clkrm., fine drawing rm., gd. dining rm., study to secluded sth. suntrap sunbathing patio & 100ft. walled gdn., lawn, weeping willow, roses, vine & "Forest of raspberries" (Cutting at end), 5 bedrms., NEW pine-panelled bathrm., lovely BIG kit./b'fast. rm., pine cpbds., units., wine cellar. Prking. 3 CARS. SACRIFICE £12,995 FHLD.

*NT*N R*DG*RS, TELY'S SCARLET PIMP, a frustrated fisherman moves towards the water. *"Any way kids growing out of attic"* leaves FASHIONABLE ISLINGTON (*"10 mins Saville"*) luxurious Regency Town House – Thousands lavished *"Everything functional AND beautiful"* Noble 25ft Drawing rm, orig marble chmnypce. *Avant garde* pine pnld super lab sav Dining/Kit, 4 Bedrms, wall of wdrbs, vanitory units. 2 new Bathrms. Small sculptoress's studio to *"Pathetic attempt at a Gdn. lawn, no more than 2 can decently sunbathe at a time."* ONLY £15,995 FHLD.

HAIRY ARCHITECT'S DRAMATIC Ent flr
MAIS superbly created from POSH PIMLICO
Period res. GORGEOUS Drawing rm. 18ft
HIGH (wall of GLASS 18ft HIGH) to Music
rm/extra Bedding-down rm. DBLE GLASS drs
to secluded Patio. FLOODLIT Gdn of interesting
growths & nearby FIG. Dining rm. 2 Bedrms.
Mod Bathrm. Lab-sav Kit, blt-in units. Lse 150
yrs. GR ONLY £10. TERRIFIC BARGAIN:
£11,995.

RESIDENCE OF DISTINCTION. Those who knew ACACIA HOUSE only as a convent may not know that the Rev. Mother ascertaining that their Patron Saint's Day coincided with the birthday of Mr SEAN CONNERY, graciously allowed him to take over. Now, with Vacant Possession, he MUST SELL this fine detached great Victorian house. Secluded at end of cul-de-sac delving into the heart of ACTON PARK, W.3, it retains its air of cloistered calm, altho' the Nuns' changing-rm is now given over to Body Building appliances & a bar billiards table. Enormous but elegant 'L' Drawing-rm 35ft × 20ft. gleaming oak flr, Dining rm, sliding picture window to secluded, walled gdn. Approx. 60-ft Sq. Study. Well fit lab saving kitn. Master bedrm, dressing-rm with fine wdrbds 4 other Bedrms. 2 mod Bathrms. Nursery kit or 6th Bedrm on top flr leads to sun-bathing balcony. Laundry rm. CENTRAL HEATING. Splendid value £14,995 FHLD.

P*M*L* H*RL*W, seductive spy of The Silver Screen & Stately-Home Br*ll* P*d telyad girl, sadly leaves the groom's cottage (1855 Gothic) of Historic Coval Manor. Quiet lane E. SHEEN nr RICHMOND PK. NEW CENT HEAT/roof/ plumbing. A romantic cottage in country gdn rather gone to seed in wild profusion of hydrangea, pear, plum & apple trees. Comfortable draw rm, open f'plce. Snug din rm. 2 Bedrms. Mod B & K stainless steel sink. MARVELLOUS BARGAIN £7,500 FHLD.

£5,675 FHLD., even try offer. LIGHTWEIGHT TROUSER EXPORTER TO DARKEST AFRICA & AIR HOSTESS sacrifices lovingly reconstructed spic & span PERIOD COTTAGE, fashionable TEDDINGTON (v. nr. Studios). Lovely little drawing rm., panelled, bkshelves., attrac. dining rm., 2 DBLE bedrms. SUPER NEW k & b. CENT. HEAT. Sunbathing gdn., own veg., tree heavy with ripening peaches.

DISTINGUISHED BRASENOSE PHILOSO-PHER & PSEPHOLOGIST – made good doing those brilliant ads for slimming things – offers enchanting irregular Period Res., virgin white. FASH. ISLINGTON. Superbly modernised (money doesn't matter now): CENT HEAT. Cosy draw rm., arch to study. Pentagon din. rm., 3 bedrms., one a 24ft. top Studio rm. Secluded sun. ter. Mod. bathrm., shower. Kit. £14,758 FHLD.

THE SUPERB SPACIOUS BUCOLIC BECK-ENHAM (18 mins Vic) new '65 Architect blt res of X of the F.O. & Lady Encyclopaedist – Nigerian expert (her gynaecologist school chum of Ojukwu says he was always a nut case; but I think our govt are to blame profiteering in arms – often as not you only bruise or frighten with a knobkerry & unclothed, unconverted savages tend NOT to kill the women & kids as efficiently as we W.A.S.P.s). In old grounds, own super 100ft back gdn, flowers & pears *"edible? – hate 'em, I throw them at the children"* she says. Big parquet hall, clkrm. Elegant 1st flr Drawrm to sunbathing balcony. Splendid lge Din/Kit plus formal dining rm for black tie & petits pois. 3 DBLE Bedrms (rm for 4th). Upper class Bathrm. CENT HEAT. GARAGE. ONLY £8,450 FHLD.

DERELICT DOSS HOUSE FASHIONABLE
PIMLICO (will now only sell to gentle-people for
single-fmly) 3rd Flr: 3 Bedrms. 2nd Flr: 1 big & 1
small dble Bedrm. 1st Flr: huge 'L' draw rm over
30ft lurking behind old newspapers, quite a charming early 19th Cent chimnypce. Rm at rear wld
make bath-dress rm. Grnd Flr: 2 rms thrown into
one abt 30ft. Rear rm (grnd flr Kit?). Basement –
Horrible! (3 rms – all right. I suppose, if tarted
up. Back yard with patch of earth & an outside
lav which put the skivs firmly in their place on a
cold wet night. Dirt cheap at £12,995. Bring your
own torch.

NICE START TO THE YEAR with an almost archetypal client, scion of Wm of Orange's Court Jeweller, British Intelligence & Anglo-French Management Consultant & Writer of Espionage Thrillers – MUST SELL Spacious (lab-sav. 2 flrs) Edwardian fmly res in quiet refined rd KEW GDNS, rather well modernised with not much regard to cost. NEW CENT HEAT. Charming Draw rm. Period chmnypce, to nice Alpine Gdn. Din rm, polished flr gleaming in the candlelight. 4 gd Bedrms. Mod B & K. £11,990 Fhld.

SPACIOUS fin de siècle fmly. res. off WEST-SIDE, WANDSWORTH COMMON. Non-base lovingly modernised by successful Surveyor who, at 30, is retiring to Welsh XVI Cent. farmstead with girl nanny – "money isn't everything." Splendid 27ft. double. draw. rm. to conservatory, pretty stained glass, fine Afghan red din. rm., 5 dble. bedrms. (1 as studio, another as extra din.-kit.: for genteel lucrative sub-let?). 2 new bathrms., gd. kit. Gdn., canary creeper, giant sunflowers. TERRIFIC BARGAIN £7,990 FHLD.

FASH CAMDEN TOWN (nr Camden Sq). Res of talented young British Designer – *"Sanitary ware & costume jewelry"* – who has had tempting offer in Chicago – where he can combine the two. MUST SELL after spending thousands. Vic. Period Res. Elegant Draw rm, gleam beech flr, arch to Din/Kit, 30ft in all. 2 DBLE Bedrms, shower rm, Sunbathing terrace & 60ft Gdn of flowers. Base flat 2 rms, K & B let at £3 15s p.w. As it's not finished to the satisfaction of his perfectionist soul, sacrifice £7,675 FHLD.

FRENCH ARISTOCRAT OF PLANTAGENET DESCENT. The Viscomte de R*****, met English Air Hostess: was told that SYDENHAM was the dernier cri.: now, 4 babies later, they are returning to France & MUST SELL modernised Edwardian fmly. res. Gdn., 70 shrubs/trees, leap over wall to lovely MAYOW PARK. Lounge hall, fine spacious draw. rm, elegant din. rm., genuine Georgian chmnypce., 5 DBLE. bedrms., basins, balconies, big bathrm., big b'fast rm., kit., wine cellar. ONLY £7,600 FHLD.

THE GRADUATE – **B.A.** (Oxon). Enriched, promoting motor bikes, s. towels & washing machines. *"Made a lovely home in N. Finchley"* (Nr Tally Ho), now banished Birmingham. MUST SELL lavishly modernised Edwardian Fmly Res. New CONSTOR CENT. HEAT. Super professionally designed Draw rm to Gdn. lawn, apple, roses, sand-pit. Comfortable Din rm, 3 Bedrms, Bathrm, Bright brand-new B'fast rm, Kit. £6,600 FHLD!

FASH SOUTHSIDE CLAPHAM COMMON $\frac{1}{4}$ mile. $12\frac{1}{2}$ mins car NATIONAL THEATRE. Spacious Vic res "Room for a *real* family" says Journalist who has graduated from Furtive Amours of the Famous to Pure Science. The ample Study (where he wrote abt "Pulse Code Modulation") with big dble drs to Drawrm, to Gdn, apple, pear, lilac, roses, clematis, grass. Playrm/B'fastrm. French windows to Gdn. 2 Bathrms The Master's Mod Bathrm. 2nd utility Bathrm where French au pair & washing can be done together. Kit. Terrific value £6,995 FHLD.

PRIMROSE HILL, N.W.3 Where a white-robed Druidical virgin does something on, I think, the first day of Spring. Swinging Solicitor, Pop-Promoting, book-loving American TV Chief & Brand New Swedish Model's CHALCOT PARK Architect's Masterpiece (see Readers Digest 'photo). Impressive 31 × 17ft Draw rm. Huge picture windows & sliding ones to SUNBATHING TERRACE. Engaging spiral stair. 3 bedrms to another secluded Sunbathing Ter. 2 Lux bathrms. Super labsav kit. CENT HEAT. GARAGE. Has eye on something even grander at Windsor (didn't know it was on Market) hence give-away price £20,550.

AN ALMOST RECKLESS expenditure of money & good taste has made this the perfect pad. Fabulously fash CHELSEA (DEFOE lived up the rd). Marvellously modernised 2nd flr Mansion FLAT off CHEYNE WALK. Elegant Draw rm, arch to library *"For my most precious things"* says cultured young Solicitor – Bust of Dizzy, etc., etc. 2 Bedrms, superfit wdrbs. Mod b & k. A GIFT AT £9,650 but try ANY offer.

FASHIONABLE CHELSEA. Shalcomb St. Early Vic PERIOD RES: end of terrace – you get a bulge thrown in. 8 big & 4 smaller rms. Some drs nailed up but can see 1st flr 27ft dble Draw rm, fine Period chmnypce lurks behind hardboard. Plumbing teeny bit primitive: skiv's chamberpot-scouring-sink off landing. Surprisingly Garden has saplings & emergent corms. 51 yrs. GR £90. Sacrifice £13,995 including lino on stairs. A good position in Society will enable you to fit in here: rather than more wealth. (Suggest you take hammer with claw if you want to see all the rooms).

CHARMING new ('68) Regency Style KINGS-TON HILL Architect-blt res. 100 or so yds RICH-MOND PARK, of cultured Public Relations couple (He is still not saying what he was disguised as at STALIN'S Teheran Conference & she is properly discreet about her work for Royalty.) Ideal for middle class couple on way up who have to entertain to impress equally unimportant people who have to entertain. . . . Wide Ent Hall. PARQUET. Elegant 1st flr Draw rm super bow window whole Sth side. Din rm to balcony on which a dwarf might sun himself or take a snack. Study or 4th bedrm to long thin garden. 3 other bedrms. 2 excellent lux bathrms. Fulfit kit. GARAGE for the better sort of car. SAC-RIFICE. albeit below cost: £12,675 FHLD.

KENWOOD COTTAGE, HIGHGATE. DE-TACHED DBLE-FRONTED direct o'er High-gate Ponds & miles of HAMPSTEAD HEATH. Wireless pioneer's early 18th Cent Old Mill Farm, handy for Heath & anyone like him: "Tremendously interested in birds." CENT HEAT. Very pretty Draw rm, bay window, oak flr. Book-lined library din rm, 3 dble bedrms, wdrbs, 2 mod bathrms, shower. Wellfit lab-sav b'fast rm kit, super worktops. Storerm. Very secluded walled gdn for sunbathing. The old cowshed takes several cars &, not so long ago, a cow. £21,995 FHLD.

TUFNELL PK (Immortalised in Plomer's poem. *"A quintagenian clerk from Tufnell Park . . . his manner wld have been more uncertain, had he known that Dublin Dan, her fancy man, was behind the folkweave curtain. . . ."*). Few mins tube. Spacious Vic fmly hse. 27ft dble Draw rm, Period chmnypce. 5 Bedrms. Bathrm. B'fast rm. Vintage Kit Gdn. BARGAIN £6,500 FHLD.

HRH PRINCESS R*SP*GLS*** instructs us to sell her Town res. PECKHAM RYE. Small rather mean late Vic artisan's cottage. Dble Drawing rm. 3 Bedrms. 2 BATHRMS. Kit. All dec in cheap & rather nasty wallpaper. Horribly neglected gdn. Pear, Worcester Permain, blackberries, raspberries. *"Very neighbourly road"* says HRH. "Nice for one's children if they can get into the Trike Set." ABSURDLY CHEAP. £4,495 FHLD.

**WASH AWAY THE EXCESSES OF A PERMIS-
SIVE SOCIETY** – **tumble from your bed, lurch
down the garden (Grass & daffs) straight into the
Regents Canal. Fash Islington** – beautifully
modernised Period res. CENT HEAT. Elegant 1st
flr 27ft Draw rm to SUNBATHING Terrace o'lkg
Canal. Attractive din rm. Also additional
GRAND 30ft grnd flr Rec Rm, wld make 2
EXTRA dble bedrms. 3 other bedrms one to top
flr covered Sunterrace. Mod bathrm, shower. Big
B'fast rm. Kit with Laundry area. Great wealth
has made this fit for a Pop Singer – or Princess –
or both, yet it is no more than the cost of a nasty
comfortable suburban villa, ONLY £19,855
FHLD.

THE PRINCESS below, said she hesitated to
bring her house to us because she didn't think it
posh enough. The newly affluent middle-class is,
thank God, not the mainstay of our business &,
however, humble we are delighted to sell YOUR
House or Flat, however horrible ANYWHERE
in Gtr London (only). Scale Commission & no
need for Sole Agency.

CR*SS, former Observer Washington cor-
respondent (Had Xmas Card from Pascifist Pentagon Colonel: *"Peace on Earth"*) and author of
"Fall of the British Empire" MUST SELL Super-
lux top (8th) floor new '59 FLAT DULWICH
WOOD PARK, spacious and sunny. CENT
HEAT. LIFT. Magnificent Draw rm abt 21ft ×
17ft, bkshlves, polished mahog flr, lovely picture
window o'er treetops. 2 DBLE bedrms, fine
wdrbs. Lux bathrm & kit/din rm, dble stainless
sinks. Landscaped grnds, own GARAGE. 88 yrs.
GR £18. ONLY £6,955.

MONO-SODIUM GLUTANAMATE MAN &
TOILETRY GIRL ROMP & SUNBATHE IN
PRIVATE MEADOW – weeping willows down
to river Crane, appertaining to SPACIOUS 1st flr
Top Mais (own St Ent) small quiet new '62 select
Block end leafy cul-de-sac nr TWICKENHAM
GREEN 19 min W'loo. Underflr CENT HEAT.
Super 25ft Drawrm to Big sunbalcony. 2 dble
bedrms, wdrbs. Superfit b&k, waste disp, pine-clad
b'fast area. Excellent decor. Own GARAGE. 191
yrs. GR 12 Gns. A GIFT AT £6,800.

IMMACULATE VIRGIN-WHITE THEATRE MAN'S PERIOD res. Fash. unspoiled St Margaret's Grove, TWICKENHAM. Still enough Proles around to give the scene character. O'lkng PARKLAND & TREES (access), mini-river Crane meanders at bottom of your 70ft rather wild gdn. SUPER CENT HEAT. Delightful 24ft dble Draw rm, PARQUET, bkshlves. 3 Bedrms, wdrb. Mod bathroom. Well fit pine panld b'fast rm kit. VERY CHEAP £7,655 FHLD.

IT REALLY MEANS SOMETHING SOCIALLY TO LIVE IN A FILTHY OLD GEORGIAN HOUSE IN FASH ISLINGTON. Liverpool Rd, N.1. is one of the filthiest we have had for a long time & must be a bargain. Base: 2 rms 15 × 12 & 12 × 10. Grnd: Front rm 16 × 10 & even a bathrm! Rear: STUDIO 2 intercom rms 30ft & W.C. All a *real* artist needs. 1st flr: 2 rms wld make Grand 24 ft Draw rm. 2nd flr: 2 rms 15 × 13 & 11 × 11. Also 2 storerms. If you've ever wanted to live on the Set of a Sean O'Casey play, here's your chance. PATHETICALLY CHEAP £9,955 EVEN TRY OFFER.

COMPLETELY UNKNOWN FAMOUS RACING DRIVER'S really beautifully restored & dec PERIOD CORNER RES FASH ISLINGTON. OIL CENT HEAT. Clkrm. Elegant 27ft "L" Drawrm fine Chmnypce. Formal dinrm. 4 bedrms, wall super Wdrbds. Mod bathrm, shower. Wellfit kit. Secluded walled gdn. SACRIFICE £14,995 FHLD.

BETTER SORT OF TELY DIRECTOR (Zola & all that) & small BLONDE ACTRESS'S FASH FULHAM fmly res fabulous re-vamp by famous Architects Stout & Litchfield – thousands lavished. Drawrm leading to dinrm, elegant, comfortable, exciting, sliding wall of glass to gdn of flowers, heavy with scent of honeysuckle, clematis, runner beans, roses & love apples, lawn secluded he says *"For natural sunbathing."* A Star's luxury kit. Mod bathrm. 4 bedrms (3 DBLE). Big top one ideal Studio/Study. *"Leaning out of window o'er the trees music softly wafts from Hurlingham &, for a magic moment, the Class barrier melts & you imagine yourself there amongst the nobs."* SACRIFICE £14,510.

"A VERY ODD PROPERTY – don't notice trains anymore", says Daredevil Motorway Engineer of his DETACHED strangely secluded PERIOD RES skulking behind 8ft gates & cobbled forecourt – Privacy & Parking. N.W.6. MAIDA VALE. As 2 vacant s/c flats & gd basement workshop for making Reproduction steamrollers. Grnd flr: Draw rm. Bedrm. b&k. 1st (top) flr openplan STUDIO flat. All warm, sunny & dbleglazed. ONLY £8,995 FHLD.

WE ARE HONOURED TO BE ABLE TO OFFER THE RAJ KUMAR'S PRIVATE RESIDENCE. Like all the Raj's Residences, Exmouth Villa, TEDDINGTON (32 min train W'loo) is Gleam Virgin-White, & has space for GARAGE. Elec CENT HEAT. Ample 25ft Draw rm to patio & gdn, with exotic blooms brought from the Himalayas: known to the cognoscenti as Rhododendron & Azalla. Big 18ft Pine panld Din/kit, 2 DBLE Bedrms. Mod bathrm. TERRIFIC BARGAIN £6,475 FHLD.

FASH FOXES DALE, BLACKHEATH spacious grnd flr Super Span FLAT newly dec to taste of prosperous builder of new cinemas (For "Pale blue films") & Bank of England lady who, alas, must now sell. The spacious lovely 25ft Drawrm with cheerful open fire & extensive library shelves make it perfect for a brace of bookworms. 3 gd bedrms, fit wdrbs. Mod bathrm. Superfit kit, b'fast bar. GARAGE. Landscaped grnds, grass rear for your children. 993 yrs. GR £28. ONLY £7,995.

CHARTERED ACCOUNTANT & SURGEON'S YOUNG LIBERAL DAUGHTER OFF TO A PHOENICIAN ISLE SACRIFICE Period corner Cottage FASH CAMDEN TOWN. *Cent Heat.* Cosy Drawrm. 3 bedrms. Mod b & k. Abt couple of thousand spent but nothing flash about it. *"Really it's a pretty nasty house in many ways,"* says owner, but where else can you buy a FREEHOLD for £7,530 EVEN TRY OFFER with an address you are not ashamed to give a taxi driver. Call Sun Prowse Place, off Jeffreys St, N.W.1.

IN AN AFFLUENT SOCIETY MONEY ALONE CAN'T BUY YOU CLASS but NORTHGATE HOUSE (dating back to 1686, with Queen Anne features) HEALTHY HIGHGATE HILL has recently been the res of scion of ancient Mexican Kings. Ideal posh Professional &/or fmly use. CENT HEAT. Fine Ent Hall to *"Dome."* Elegant Stair & Study both pine panelled. 1st flr Drawrm, & din rm, both of noble proportions. 6 Gd Bedrms. Ancient bathrm (rm for more). 3 showerrms. Big kit. Wonderful 180ft walled garden of flowers, interesting trees. Nice warm wine cellar. WONDERFUL VALUE £28,000 FHLD.

FASH ISLINGTON BRILLIANT BEARDE
ACADEMIC UPPER-CLASS ARCHITECT
beautifully restored & modernised Period res
Regency manner (circa 1840) few min Oxford Ci
cus & City. CENT HEAT. Clkrm. Fine 27ft db
Drawrm: shelves for *"Good books & object d'art*
Dinrm/playrm/Study. 3 bedrms. Mod bathrr
Din-Kit beautifully fit, twin steel sinks &c to su
drenched patio for b'fast. Immac decor. Attracti
walled gdn, mountain ash. ONLY £11,855.

DR X THE ELECTRIC FENIAN PSYCHIA-
TRIST & GIRL ACTRESS OFFERS CHARM-
ING REGENCY HANGOVER 1840 Period res,
leafy countrified rd PUTNEY. Thousands lavished with exquisite sensibility. CENT. HEAT.
Gleaming waxed flrs. Clkrm. Most charming 28ft
dble Drawrm, shuttered windows, bookshelves &
blazing open fire. Dr is particularly proud of Billiards rm altho' baize bit rugged & only one cue –
pour le sport; make a formal dinrm – port is still
passed round on Putney Hill. 3 DBLE bedrms.
Mod bathrm. Delightful b'fastrm/kit. Secluded
walled sunbathing gdn, lilac, Russian vine, clematis & honeysuckle. WONDERFUL BARGAIN
£14,505 FHLD.

THE SKIN-DIVING VET & UNUSED GIRL
ACTRESS SACRIFICE (By CRYSTAL
PALACE WOODS & NR. DULWICH) LARGE
DETACHED VICTORIAN (circa 1865) HOUSE
WITH STRANGE OBSERVATION TOWER:
look down on your neighbours or lift your eyes
to the distant Downs. As 2 spacious mais but vac
poss a BIG fmly Res. Ent mais: Elegant Drawrm.
Study. Super living/din rm to mod kit, 2 DBLE
Bedrms, ENORMOUS new bathrm. UPPER
MAIS. Delightful 24ft dble Drawrm with arch. 3
gd bedrms b & k, b'fast rm. Sunbathing (if you
shift around a bit), gdn of roses, lawn & gorgeous
"Protected" Cedar. ONLY £8,555 FHLD.

TORY PARTY AGENT GOING INTO
FRUIT & VEG *"Less neurotic than Party members – even a wilting cabbage"* FORCED SACRI-
FICE much loved Fulham fmly home for 40 yrs.
Front parlour, fine plastered ceiling. Dinrm (4th
bedrm) to small gdn, grass, roses, asparagus gone
over to nature. 3 bedrms (1 enormous), $\frac{1}{2}$ tiled
bathrm, b'fast rm. Sep kit. ONLY £8,995 FHLD.

B. WH*T*L*W, Star of Silver Screen's beautifully modernised Vic fmly Riverside res: bought for sentimental reasons – Sir Pelham (Plum) Warner selected his bowlers on the lawns. DATCHET, BUCKS. Gorgeous big Garden, plum, figs & apple, enormous horse chestnut, summerhouse, BOATHOUSE, 60ft river frontage, BRAND NEW MOORING, uninterrupted views over the private grnds to WINDSOR CASTLE. Short walk Stn, M4 3 mins by car. CENT HEAT, DBLE GLAZING. Attractive reception/din hall. Spacious elegant drawrm, open log fire, to gdn. Study/playrm, concealed blt-in beds. 3 bedrms, superb fit wdrbs. Master bedrm has secret shower with bidet. SUPER SUNNY B'FAST RM TO TERRACE & BIG WINDOW O'ER GDN. Lab-sav kit. Laundryrm with child's w.c. Carport several cars. ONLY £18,950 FHLD.

LADY DIRECTOR of Council Estate Theatre Workshop (Even Skinheads transmogrified by Creative Art – now referred to as *"That calm, peaceful lot"*) offers her FASH CAMDEN TOWN delightful dble-fronted 19th cent Period res o'lkng REGENTS CANAL, quiet crescent; pedestrians only. Lovingly modernised. Nightstore & Dimplex CENT HEAT. Watch boats sail by from interesting 1st flr Drawrm, mahogany flr. 2 bedrms, 1 as Study. Mod bathrm, b'fastrm kit PLUS light base FLAT Bedsit, kit, 2nd MOD BATHRM. FULL vac poss. ONLY £9,999. FHLD.

BLACKHEATH quietly affluent priv tree-lined rd where a Poetry Award rates higher than a Jag – or even a Bentley. Richly appointed fmly RES Architect blt '64 for ex-RAF Hawker Hart type. CENT HEAT. Gleam costly PARQUET. 22ft. Drawrm: folding drs open to Hall & Study/-Playrm form wizard Party rm. 4 bedrms, walls of wdrbs, view of Heath. Lux tiled bathrm. Super b'fast kit, fit Dishwasher. Walled gdn of roses. GARAGE. SACRIFICE £13,995 FHLD.

NO LESS CULTURED BLACKHEATH. The spacious immaculate & absolutely charming Top (2nd) flr FLAT of Top P.R. couple – she: Copywriter; deodorant chocolate & the Labour Party. He: Recruitment for the Army. "Thanks to the violence in N. Ireland the Army is getting an encouraging enlistment of skinheads" (For those who are teetering on the edge of protest: I am on the side of the army & would rather see the bigots at the top fight it out amongst themselves in a bearpit. REB). Anyway spacious cosy drawrm has wall of bookshelves, gd dble bedrm, a wall of fit cpbds. LUX bathrm, bidet, shower, vanitory unit. Superfit diningrm/kit. Intimate communal sunbathing patio, lawn, trees & flowers. ABSURDLY CHEAP £5,455 EVEN TRY ANY OFFER INC FIT CARPET, SUPER COOKER & FRIG.

CHARTERED ACCOUNTANT & SURGEON'S LIBERAL YOUNG DAUGHTER SACRIFICE PERIOD corner COTTAGE FASH CAMDEN TOWN. CENT HEAT. Cosy Drawrm. 3 Bedrms. Mod. b&k. Abt couple of thousand spent but nothing flash about it. *"Really it's a pretty nasty house in many ways"* says owner, but where else can you buy a FHLD for £6,995 EVEN TRY OFFER.

£6,755 FHLD TRY ANY OFFER (from) HORRIBLE HOUSES IN W.14. P. G. WODEHOUSE once wrote that when people woke up aesthetically, & artists & architects went round with burning brands – W. Ken would be the first to fall. *par example:* Vic cottage; 5 rms & kit. Outside latrine, & bath hanging on the outhouse wall. Bit of gdn with a little struggling plant life: £7,755 FHLD TRY ANY OFFER (This one's quite respectable inside). Others from £6,755 FHLD.

£6,550 FHLD TRY ANY OFFER! All too solidly blt fin de siecle fmly res. "Not too desperately ugly" said University Lecturer in Psychology who has come to terms with life. "A Freudian might like it." Modernised & produces abt £1,100 p.a. as 4 furnished flats/flatlets: cld revert. Drawrm. Formal Dinrm/Library/5th bedrm. 4 Bedrms. 13ft 8 B'fast rm. Mod b & k. Glazed sunrm to gdn, overgrowth lawn, flowers, plum tree. Green vista o'er Playing Flds. 2 min walk Stn LEYTONSTONE. 16 min L'pool St, 27 min Oxford Circus.

HISTORIC FLAT, W.1. "2 stones' throw from EROS." Super 4th flr. FLAT (LIFT) quietly tucked away in Theatreland. Converted with discretion, preserving the pretty arched windows, from private rooms of famous, respectable fin de siecle Restaurant "It was alright to take a Lady to PAGANIS" His Grace, The Bishop of X. Cosy drawrm., dinrm. and super fit. kit., seats 10. 2 gd. bedrms., bathrm. The supersonic March of Time cannot match the Style, comfort & cringing service once enjoyed by the aristocracy, gentry & clergy. We hope this flat goes to someone who can appreciate the atmosphere. ONLY £4,995. Pres. lse. to Dec., '75. £35 p.a.

SH*R*D*N M*RL*Y'S Sunny extremely wellfit new '65 Peckarmans Wood, Sydenham Hill res access/o'lkng woods to DULWUCH WOODS only 13 min Vic so it's possible after an evening telly-stint of the mediocre, sadism & trash to cleanse the palate & refresh the intellect with *"Late Night Line-up"* – & still get 8 hrs sleep. CENT HEAT. Clkrm. Spacious elegant 1st flr Drawrm o'er woods, extra windows, gleam mahogany flrs. Dinrm to balcony, 4 bedrms, wdrbds Lux b & k. Own gdn plus use wooded grnds beyond. GARAGE. 93 yrs. GR £50 ONLY £11,505.

COSY GARCONNIERE OF THE TARZAN
OF GLADSTONE PARK, N.W.10. This crudite
wrestler & Man of Letters (6 books to his credit)
& beautiful yogagirl have tastefully embellished
comfortable mod '30's res. "*Marble Arch* 12 *min
in the E Type*." Nightstore HEAT. Attractive
Drawrm, dble drs to Dirtrm form MAGNIFI-
CENT 32ft Pine panelled Romping – or formal
Reception Rm to Gdn of flowers & SUN-
BATHING LAWN. 3 Bedrms, ½ tiled bathrm.
WRIGHTON kit/bfastrm. 2 CAR GARAGE.
ONLY £8,479 FHLD.

LAMBETH. FASHIONABLE ADDRESS with just enough proles to do the dirty work, give the place character & keep food prices low. Lady from The Office of Works & Gentleman whose firm built the first flying machine to cross the Atlantic, an all wood hand-cranked washing machine, have, for 30 yrs., lovingly preserved this spotless fin de siecle Fmly. Res. Draw. rm., comfortable din. rm., 5 bedrms., dress. rm. or single bedrm., bathrm., tiny nursery kit., b'fastrm., kit. to paved gdn. 2 warm inside lavs. & a perfectly good servants' one – outside. AN AWFUL LOT OF HOUSE FOR NOT MUCH MONEY. £8,255 FHLD. TRY ANY OFFER.

£7,550 **FHLD TRY ANY OFFER.** FABULOUSLY FASH. FULHAM. It is hard to say which is the most unprepossessing, the house or the situation? It is, at least, convenient for Lots Road Power Stn and with no Govt having a sense of style & an increasingly dreadful environment it is still possible for persons to make their personal pads passable. Edwardian fmly res. Gnd flr: Sitting rm., 2 bedrms, b'fast rm., Kit. Small gdn. 1st flr; Pleasant Sitting rm abt 18ft., 2 DBLE Bedrms., Kit. with sink, bath, Ascot & steps down for dinner guests who wish to stroll in gdn after dinner. (See illustration on front cover)

FABULOUSLY FASH PIMLICO. Wonderful opportunity to secure this DESIRABLE RESIDENCE which has everything – dry rot, a settlement, filthy decor, running cold water – sometimes where it was intended, the soft glow of gas lighting & general air of decay which is irresistible to the softened scions of the bourgeoisie, who have never had it so good/bad. Basemnt: Front rm, damp wall & tiled slab chimneypce. Back addition rm with bath & geyser. Grnd Flr: Front rm with ceiling rose & original chmnypce. Small kit with aboriginal mini range. 1st Flr: "L" Drawrm with intercommunicating doors & original chimneypces painted over. 2nd Flr: Front dble bedrm with a hole in the ceiling. Rear single Bedrm. Tiny garden with struggling sycamore; indicating that nature can overcome the folly of man – maybe. SACRIFICE £14,500. 80 yrs. G.R. £90. Sayed Yousuf Mahmoud Bey will graciously admit you on Sun between 2.30 & 5.

FABULOUSLY FASH LENNOX GDNS, S.W.1. between KNIGHTSBRIDGE & Sloane Sq. WIZARD 4th Top Flr. FLAT of Film Producer, Group Capt. X, DSO, DFC, AFC, who graduated from filming Heinkels and Dorniers with a wing camera to *"a more hazardous job – female Film Stars – not so easily shot down ..."* No lift – per ardua, ad astra. Interesting 30ft Drawrm, tons of light, windows both ends, o'lkng rather super GARDEN SQUARE. Dble Bedrm, 2 walk-in closets as dressing rms. Tiled bathrm, Shower. Dinrm/Kit. Decor all a bit dim. FANTASTIC BARGAIN £10,995.

D*SM*ND W*LC*X: MAN – by the grace of God – ALIVE, moving 150 yards nearer Studio, SACRIFICES splendid mod interwar DETACHED dble-fronted res KEW GDNS, RICHMOND view of Pagoda. CENT HEAT. Attractive Drawrm, solid brick-blt bar has supported many deviating actors & journalists. Dinrm, recessed shelves for books & objets d'art. Restful SOUND-PROOFED Study to SUNRM, French windows to very pleasant Gdn. Lawn, Croquet, flowers, Willow & *"over-sexed Peach."* 4 Gd Bedrms, basins, SUPERFIT WALL OF WDRBS. LUXURY pine panelled *"Blue"* Bathrm, BIDET. SUPER pine panelled b'fastrm & SUPERFIT KIT. GARAGE. ABSURDLY CHEAP £16,999 FHLD.

DID HER BIT DURING THE WAR BUT STILL CAPABLE OF GIVING A GOOD TIME – PROVIDING YOU DON'T GO TOO FAR –say Skindles. Le Touquet might be risky – Bermuda a disaster. Altho' God knows Columbus made it without a Gardner 4LW (overhauled '71, new fuel tanks, lines & filters, 8½ knots, range 700 miles). Beautifully blt as PLEASURE YACHT "SUNBEAM VIII" in '28, pitch pine on oak & rock elm. 56ft mainly 7ft headrm. 9ft 6 dinghy 40 + Seagull o'bd. SALOON with berth, Rayburn back boiler, bkshelves, china cabinets. Engine rm, workbench. Wheelhse 2 berths, all controls. P4 Compass, Searchlight, Foghorn range 1½ miles. With all that glass it's a super sunrm. 3 Bedrms, wdrbs, dresstbles. Mod bathrm. Galley, stainless sink, 4 burner cooker, eye level grill, pts for frig & spindryer. Bucolic Mooring Hampton Wick, Kingston. 20 min W'loo, £12 a month. COLLOSSAL BARGAIN £5,999 TRY ANY OFFER.

HOW ROMANTIC TO DWELL IN GROUNDS OF THRALE HALL where Dr JOHNSON strolled with Mrs. T. "The woman had a bottom of good sense . . . I say the woman was *fundamentally sensible*." Here, in Thrale Rd. STREATHAM, is an excellent 1910 fmly res in very good condition. Bec Common end of Rd. CENT HEAT. Attractive Drawrm, roaring open fire, dr to gdn plethora peaches, elderberry, honeysuckle, fig & outside W.C. Large Study or Formal Dinrm. A 15ft Din/b'fastrm. 5 Bedrms, 4 DBLE. Plus VAST LOFT: ideal au pair romping rm/conversion STUDIO. Kit. GARAGE with access to rear lane *"Right of way for horsedrawn fire appliance"* ABSURDLY CHEAP £9,505 FHLD.

THE RED HOUSE, LITTLE MAPLESTEAD. Essex/Suffolk border 75 mins train Lon. Comfortable detached REGENCY RES of N*CH*L*S T*ML*N whose prescient S. Times article ('65?) "ZAPPING THE CONG" told of helicopter ride with a blood-thirsty American General who enjoyed killing: irresponsibly taking pot shots at people. . . . ACRE ramshackle but potentially glorious gdn, orchard. Croquet Lawn. Big rms, nice bow windows infinitely peaceful now U.S. Base at Wethersfield closed. Oil-fired CENT HEAT. Out-buildings inc STUDIO & GARAGE. 4 Bedrms (one dormitory divisible into 2). Upper class Bathrm. Big Drawrm. Decent Dinrm. B'fast rm. Fine cosy brick flr. kit. 2 staircases for playing sardines. Absurdly cheap £11,995 FHLD.

MANOR HOUSE. Superior PURLEY. Most splendid big DETACHED 1916 MAGNIFICENTLY-blt fmly. res. of baby star of Beauty & the Beast – says she was the former & successful composer of meaningful popsongs. Set in GORGEOUS woodland setting $\frac{2}{3}$ GORGEOUS grnds. Silent pool deep with strange fish, fountain cascade, tennis court, romping sunbathing lawn, wonderful life-giving fir trees. Marvellous BIG reception hall with super bar, can cope with 50 heavy drinkers at a time. Parties of up to 200 in lovely drawrm., parquet for waltzing. Dinrm. to cope with richest repasts. A quiet Library Study. 5 cosy secluded bedrms. A properly fit. bathrm. Quiet soothing b'fastrm., kit. with dble.-stainless sink, equipped to cope with countless free-loaders. All this & heaven for £24,955 FHLD.

ONE OF A HANDSOME PAIR of 19th Cent
PERIOD HOUSES, BENBOW ROAD, HAM-
MERSMITH (named after the witty working-
class Admiral. *"The bloody liar – he told me it was
his leg not his head"* said Benbow to the surgeon
who berated him. In heat of battle he hadn't no-
ticed the cannonball which decapitated the legless
shipmate he was carrying down to the sick bay).
Clkrm. 2 intercommunicating Reception rms, folding drs, original chmnypce, abt 30ft. pleasant
Dinrm. 5 Bedrm. B'fast rm/study/extra bedrm?
Kit. walled Gdn. Not smart but cherished fmly
home for 35 yrs. Bargain £10,500 FHLD.

A RICH BUSINESS MAN'S PARADISE.
ABANDON YOURSELF TO NATURE IN
EALING, W.5. Wade waist-high thro' lush vegeta-
tion – also gone to seed – in 116ft Gdn. BIG DE-
TACHED VIC FMLY RES. Splendid Drawrm
over 20ft. beautiful cornice & chmnypce. Fine
Dinrm. Study. 5 Bedrms 2 Bathrms. B'fast/Kit. 3
GARAGES & Dove Cote Decor fashionably
squalid. Colossal Bargain £18,505 FHLD.

**A FORMER HEADMASTER OF KINGSTON
GRAMMAR SCHOOL,** Dr THOMAS
BROWN, MA. (Oxon) RESIGNED BECAUSE
HE FOUND IT *"Too far from the whores in
Town"* Now, 20 min W'loo & fast by car to W.
End at night, KINGSTON HILL still enjoys buco-
lic pleasures of RICHMOND PARK & River. A
BRACE OF NEW LUXURY 10th flr PENT-
HOUSES, Lakehouse House. There really is a
lake in beau landscaped gdns, & o'looks Coombe
Wood Golf Course. CENT HEAT &, I hope, a
Lift. Clkrm. Excellent 24ft Drawrm, spiral stair
to SUPERB 24ft Rooftop Room to Big 21 × 21ft
ROOF TERRACE. 2 DBLE Bedrms, superfit
wdrbs. Lux Bathrm, looking-glass wall. Big fulfit
b'fast/kit. GARAGE av. Look down on your
neighbours for ONLY £12,255 & £13,505 try
ANY offer. Lse 96 yrs. G.R. £40.

GRANBY HOUSE FULHAM; not only fash
but reeking with upper-class trendiness. Fin-de-
siecle FMLY RES of fun-loving Commuterman
BA Trinity *"hot-foot from China danced all night"*
& Impressionist girl painter who have really well
modernised. Directly o'erlooking BISHOP'S
PARK & gnds of FULHAM PALACE: the last
bastion of Aristocratic 18th Century hedonism.
CENT HEAT. Elegant Drawrm, Dinrm, fine
cornice & chmypce. STUDY or extra Bedrm
(expect middle-class buyer will shove a colour telly
in here). 4 Bedrms cpbds. basin. Nursery Kit or
extra Bedrm. 2 MOD BATHRMS. B'fastrm/Kit.
You can separate top floor for genteel lucrative
sub-letting. GARDEN of limp lettuce. SAC-
RIFICE £13,999 FHLD.

"Roy Brooks sold my boat in 1965 for £1,000. There's no way I can describe 'Amanda'. She had to be seen. She was a hybrid, and old ship's lifeboat which had been built up in the most primitive way. A few years later she went down with all hands – on a milk bottle! She used to settle on the mud and on this occasion – a milk bottle holed her. There was no attempt to refloat her, she was just towed away."

DAVID OWEN

"Thinking of Roy I remember first a moustache and behind it an air of friendly amusement, a candour without malice. His advertisements made our Sundays in the 50's and 60's, a sun-dappled clearing in the hideous thickets of Estate Agents prose.

GEORGE MELLY

"I can think of no better reminder of the power and force of Roy Brooks' personality than to re-read the advertising style with which he tackled the phoniness of his own profession. What's more, the property buying and selling public endorsed him over and over again, welcoming him as a thirst crazed stranger in a desert might welcome the sight of an oasis.
In a profession gilded with euphemisms and literary manipulations – actually the cover up for deceit and lies – Roy Brooks told the truth, spoke outrageously and grew successful because of it. Other estate agents, elegant and languid or urgent and hustling must have hated him. I read his advertisements as one would read jolly postcards from impudent friends who always give you the unvarnished facts in an amusing manner.

DESMOND WILCOX

"Roy Brooks was to estate dealing what Gerard Hoffnung was to music – unique and thus irreplaceable. For me Roy's column was as much a part of London as Bernard Levin's 'Taper' reviews of the House of Commons debates in The Spectator."

HUMPHREY BURTON

"Back from Korea in the fifties – when Foreign Correspondents were facing intimation of mortality as a fading breed – I met Roy Brooks while doing a BBC radio programme about property. He was already a London character, and instantly likeable.

Afterwards I spent many agreeable evenings in the surprisingly grotty garden – basement – flat in Gledhow Gardens, SW5 (suit shambolic family) where he and Barbara daily fed-and-watered a varied gathering of people-around-town; indeed one pre-Clean Air November night when the fog had come down I slept on his sitting room floor along with a Hollywood heart-throb and a bit-actor soon to be famous as Steptoe ... while Barbara went into her mother hen routine.

Roy was a life-enhancer with an enthusiasm for all the right things and outspoken outrage at what he believed wrong. We shared a passion for Bentleys, and he stopped me buying a coach-built one-off that was cheap but somehow ... not quite right: 'If it worries you now, it'll annoy you more every time you see it'.

As the years progressed they moved up to a modern all-glass country-home creation in the Thames Valley; I often wondered how he might have described it ... This was where I saw him last. He seemed more at home amid the Kensington chaos.

I never bought a property from Roy, but with that charm and easy laughter he would have been a hard man to resist ... Ah yes, I remember him well."

ALAN WHICKER

"One of the minor delights of the 1960's was turning to the Roy Brooks' 'houses for sale' advertisements each week. Amazingly, huge numbers of readers did this, even when they were not in the market for a new home themselves. Which just goes to show that, with a little humour and imagination, normally humdrum routine business transactions can be turned into entertaining diversions. Sadly there are far too few Roy Brooks about in commerce today.

DESMOND MORRIS